Sources in Sociology
A Workbook for GCSE

Christopher Townroe
George Yates

Longman

LONGMAN GROUP UK LIMITED
Longman House, Burnt Mill, Harlow, Essex CM20 2JE, UK and Associated Companies throughout the World.

© **Longman Group UK Limited 1989**
*All rights reserved; no part of this publication
may be reproduced, stored in a retrieval system,
or transmitted in any form or by any means, electronic,
mechanical, photocopying, recording, or otherwise,
without the prior written permission of the Publishers.*

*First published 1989
ISBN 0 582 03337 3*

Set in 10/13pt Times, Linotron 202

*Produced by Longman Group (Far East) Ltd
Printed in Hong Kong*

British Library Cataloguing in Publication Data
*Townroe, Christopher
  Sources in sociology: a workbook for GCSE.
  1. Sociology. Research
  I. Title II. Yates, George
  301'.072*

ISBN 0-582-03337-3

For Susannah and Georgina

Contents

Introduction	5
1 Research methods	**8**
Kerry Hinsby's GCSE project	8
Kerry's project continued	10
Studies using mixed methods	12
Sampling	14
An example of a questionnaire	16
2 Gender roles	**18**
Body images	18
Socialisation	20
Women in restaurants	21
Gender and schooling	22
Women and work	24
Feminism and the demands of the women's movement	26
3 Youth and old age	**27**
Rites of passage	27
Changing childhood and youth	28
British youth cults	30
Youth cults – a crazy phase?	32
People not 'pensioners'	34
4 The family	**36**
Changes in family life	36
Types of families	38
Caring for relatives	40
Divorce	42
Gender roles in Britain and the USSR	44
5 Rural and urban communities	**46**
Rural life	46
Housing patterns	48
High-rise flats	50
6 Racism	**52**
Types of racism	52
Ethnic minorities in the police and civil service	54
Opportunities and the future	56
7 Education	**58**
The curriculum	58
Schools do matter	60
Private education	62
8 Social stratification	**64**
Two types of stratification	64
Aspects of class in Britain	66
Changes in the class structure	68
Class in the USSR	70
9 Religion	**72**
Religion and social control	72
Secularisation	74
Religious cults	76

Contents

10 The media — **78**
Violence and the media — 78
Political bias in the press — 80
Elections and the media — 82
The ownership of the media — 84

11 Politics — **86**
Pressure groups — 86
Gypsy site simulation — 88
The 1987 General Election — 90

12 Deviance and crime — **92**
Deviance — 92
Juvenile delinquency — 94
The process of policing — 96

13 Wealth and poverty — **98**
The rich and the poor — 98
Unemployment and poverty — 100
Poverty and health — 102

14 Work and leisure — **104**
What is work and how is it changing? — 104
Occupations — 106
Working conditions, leisure and class — 108
The trade unions — 110

Answers and acknowledgements — **112**

Introduction

We have compiled this book with three aims in mind:

1 Complementing your introductory textbook
This book is for use with textbooks which introduce sociology, such as *Sociology for GCSE* by Christopher Townroe and George Yates, Longman 1987.

We hope that the extracts in this book will provoke interest in and discussion on the different areas of your GCSE syllabus.

2 Suggesting research ideas
This book contains numerous research suggestions. In each case we have suggested a hypothesis: a question or theory to be investigated and tested. And in each case we have also suggested a research method. These suggestions may lead straight on to activities or they may be used to form the basis of coursework assignments or projects.

3 Testing skills
We hope that this book will enable students to practise the different skills which are required by their syllabus. Most GCSE sociology courses aim to foster the following skills:

- the ability to recognise, locate and understand relevant data from different types and sources of evidence;
- the ability to select, extract or summarise information;
- the ability to analyse and interpret evidence;
- the ability to evaluate source material.

The value of source material

There are four questions you need to ask when considering the value and usefulness of extracts of source material.

1 Where does the source material come from?
Page 6 is taken from the *New Internationalist*, March 1988. It attempts to demolish '6 Housework Myths' by giving evidence from eleven different sources. These sources are listed in the footnotes at the foot of the page.

Students should ask themselves the following sorts of questions when confronted with an extract:

- Is this a personal view?
- Is this taken from a textbook?
- Is this taken from a primary piece of original research?
- Is this information from official statistics? (for which year?)

2 What is the wider sociological context of the extract?
Here one is asking what is the relevance of the source material. To which sociological concepts and areas of debate does it refer?

We repeat that this book is a 'reader' of extracts, intended to complement but not replace the use of a standard textbook. Where extracts focus on issues such as the 'extended' or 'symmetrical' family, explanation of such concepts can be found in any introductory textbook.

Housework Myths

1. Labour-saving devices save time

In the 1920s women in the US spent an average of 60 hours a week doing housework. By the 1970s housework was taking up even *more* time: an average of 70 hours a week[1]. In 1925, when most clothes were washed by hand, women spent 5.5 hours a week doing the laundry. After the invention of the washing-machine the time had gone *up* to 6.25 hours[2]. By 1982 80 per cent of UK households owned a washing machine and 95 per cent had a vacuum cleaner, but women are doing more housework than ever[3]. This is because families change their clothes more often, expect a cleaner house and a more varied diet – and because today's mother gets practically no help from the rest of the household.

2. Cleaning keeps germs away

Housewives spend an average of two hours a day just cleaning. One study found that they clean the bath and the toilet, vacuum the living room and dust the house at least once a day[4]. But there is no evidence that anything other than extremely rudimentary house-cleaning has any effect on the health of the inmates – apart from increasing asthmatic attacks in women during bouts of dusting[1].

3. Housewives make the best mothers

Children of women with jobs outside the home are less likely to be delinquent than children of full-time housewives[5]. There are also some indications that babies are more likely to be battered by housewives than by women with jobs outside the home[5] and that housewives are themselves more likely to be battered by their husbands than women in paid employment[6]. Moreover the involvement of a caring *father* has been found to be the most important factor in preventing delinquency[5].

4. Housewives have lots of free time

Men have an average of 33.5 hours of free time per week, compared with 24.6 hours for women[7]. Even at weekends, while men and children relax, housewives work an average of six hours each day[2].

5. Housework is natural for women

Hunting is no more natural to men than housework is to women. In one study of 224 different traditional cultures, there were 13 in which women hunted and 60 in which they fished. House-building was an exclusively female occupation in 36 cultures, while there were five in which men did all the cooking and a further 38 in which cooking was routinely done by either sex[8]. In parts of Indonesia and Zaire it is the father who is expected to care for his infant child[5].

6. Men are beginning to help

Married men in the US now do *six* per cent more housework than 20 years ago[9]. Only 55% of UK men in one survey had washed the dishes at all in the previous week[10]. One in four women in another UK survey said their husbands were more of a hindrance than a help[4]. No reliable study has ever estimated men's share of the housework at anything more than 1.5 hours a day[11].

Illustrations: Jim Needle

[1] B Ehrenreich and D English, *For Her Own Good*, Pluto, UK, 1979. [2] J Vanek, *Time Spent in Housework*, Scientific American, November 1974. [3] W Faulkner and E Arnold, *Smothered by Invention*, Pluto, UK, 1985. [4] *The 1,001 Dirt Report*. [5] A Oakley, *Housewife*, Penguin, 1976. [6] R E Dobash and R Dobash, *Violence Against Wives*, Open Books, London, 1980. [7] HMSO, *Social Trends* 1987. [8] G P Murdock, *Comparative Data on the Division of Labour by Sex*, Social Forces, 1937. [9] S A Hewlett, *A Lesser Life: The Myth of Women's Liberation*, Michael Joseph, London, 1987. [10] The Association of Market Survey Organizations, UK, *Men and Domestic Work*. [11] R Cowan, *More Work for Mother*.

Introduction

3 What is the strength and adequacy of the evidence?

One needs to consider how far an extract usefully contributes to our understanding of sociological issues. A major question to pose is how far does the source material show the values, the beliefs or the prejudices of the author?

For evidence to be of greater use than opinion, it should be based on systematic observation which has been subjected to careful and critical analysis. The value of evidence is reduced if it shows deficiencies such as gaps, inconsistencies and bias.

We can assess evidence partly by drawing on our wider knowledge and our personal experience. We can also ask questions such as:

- What further sorts of evidence would help to give a fuller, more valid and balanced picture of the truth? Can alternative avenues of inquiry be suggested?
- Has any awkward or conflicting evidence been overlooked or deliberately omitted?
- What other evidence would be useful for purposes of comparison?

4 How reliable is the source material?

In considering whether the evidence is dependable, whether it can be trusted, we need to look at two issues:

(a) We must again ask what sort of source material it is:
  - Is it comment in which the author is merely expressing a feeling, an impression or an opinion?
  - Is it a body of facts which are based on observation and research?
  - Could we test the findings by repeating the investigation?
(b) How was the research conducted? If it was a survey,
  - where and when was it carried out?
  - how was it carried out? what sort of questions were asked? how were they put?
  - how large was the sample? how was it selected? was it representative?

Conclusion

Finally, we suggest three general questions to repeat as you use this book:

1 To which areas of sociological debate do the source materials refer?
2 Can I think of my own research suggestions, with my own hypotheses and research methods?
3 What is my evaluation of this group of extracts?

1 Research methods

Kerry Hinsby's GCSE project

Kerry Hinsby

Kerry Hinsby is a pupil at Walthamstow School for Girls. During her fifth year she carried out a study of 'stress in nursing' for her Sociology GCSE project. The following extracts are taken from it.

Section A: The hypothesis

The aim of my assignment is to test this hypothesis: 'Casualty nursing is a stressful occupation'.

I have completed my assignment in association with a friend who was interested in the same idea. We have written up our results separately. On 6 November 1987 we made an initial visit to the Accident and Emergency Department at Whipps Cross Hospital. We gained permission to study the nursing staff at this hospital. The head nurse was most helpful and was pleased to learn that further original research was being carried out in this area. Her support was essential, otherwise the success of our study would have been limited. That day, we gained some relevant background information. Also, we arranged to return on 18 November to study a particular nurse, perform an in-depth interview, complete a survey and generally observe the nurses within the Accident and Emergency Department.

Section B: The four research methods used

1 Secondary research
Initially I did a considerable amount of reading in order to gain a firm understanding of stress. This was obviously necessary if I was to carry out my investigation in a knowledgeable manner.

2 Questionnaire
We conducted a survey to provide representative information about the nurses.

3 Participant observation
We chose this method as we felt it would provide revealing insights into nursing. After experiencing the casualty ward for myself I am able to write with increased understanding – there is no better substitute than experience. Although, as the day at the hospital wore on it was increasingly difficult to remain objective and record my findings without bias.

4 In-depth interview
We used an in-depth interview to go beyond statistics and learn about real personal feelings. This expanded and deepened our understanding. I used an unstructured format to achieve a more extensive response. This method may not be entirely reliable but it did produce detailed information about the way people actually feel.

Section C: Secondary research

This list provides information on occupational mortality. The numbers are standardised mortality rates and 100 is the average.

Electrical engineers	145
Occupational therapists	134
Pharmacists	116
Nurses	112
Police officers	109
	Average
Authors, journalists	94
Clergy	76
University teachers	49

After looking at this table, I realised that nursing is a career with a 12 per cent above average mortality level. As I am attempting to find out whether nursing is a stressful job such secondary information is useful; it can be compared with my own findings.

I had to use medical textbooks to learn about stress and, in particular, about the symptoms of stress. Below, are some of these symptoms:

pupils dilate;
insomnia;
blood vessels near the skin contract, giving a lethargic appearance;
secretion from the sweat glands increases.

(from *Nursing Times*, Vol. 84, no. 11, 16 March 1988)

Data-response questions

1 Using Section A: what did Kerry and her friend arrange on their first visit to the hospital?
2 Using Section B:
   (a) Why do you think that Kerry found it difficult to remain objective when carrying out participant observation?
   (b) What does Kerry mean by the statement, 'we used an in-depth interview to go beyond statistics and learn about real feelings'?
   (c) Explain fully why it was important for Kerry to carry out some secondary research.
3 Explain the difference between primary and secondary research.
4 What are the advantages and disadvantages of structured and unstructured interviews?

Discussion

1 Which groups in society would be best studied by using participant observation?
2 What problems may arise as a result of relying on secondary sources such as crime figures or official suicide figures?

Research suggestion

Hypothesis: The majority of pupils find written examinations a less stressful experience than producing assessed coursework.
Method: Conduct a survey, using a variety of methods, of a representative sample of students.

Kerry's project continued

Section A: Participant observation

We began our participant observation at 10.30 am and finished at 3.30 pm. We were situated in the 'walking wounded' side, a term used to describe the minor accidents, the other side being for emergency cases. Before our visit we had made ourselves knowledgeable on the subject of stress so that we could recognise signs of it. We were not allowed to follow the nurses whilst they were actually treating patients as patients obviously want privacy when being treated. So we could only study the reception nurses whose job was to make a brief initial examination and assess the degree of injury and then refer each patient for treatment.

In general, at the beginning of each shift nurses were fresh-faced, energetic and happy looking. But after four hours of being on duty they began to show significant signs of stress, such as dilated pupils, strained features and fatigue. At this stage the nurses were becoming fidgety and irritable. Despite this, they were professional towards the patients and always had a helpful smile.

Although our day was relatively quiet, I had first-hand experience of the atmosphere in the waiting room. I felt very self-conscious and as if everyone was watching me which made relaxing difficult. I shared my feelings with a nurse, who said that being constantly on view made it difficult for her to relax.

In conclusion, nurses definitely showed signs of experiencing stress, although this would not be obvious to anyone who was unaware of the symptoms. I was becoming increasingly irritated by the demands of the patients even though these demands were not being directed at me.

Was I under stress?

Before we arrived I was quite nervous and tense. I knew that the head nurse was helpful but was unsure how the other nurses would react to us. I found the day very stressful and by the end of it I was tired and solemn. I was full of thought and much more serious than usual, which was a mood I found difficult to change. I also had a headache and a strong desire to scream to expel all my emotions. I was very relieved that the day was over.

Section B: The answers to one of the survey questions

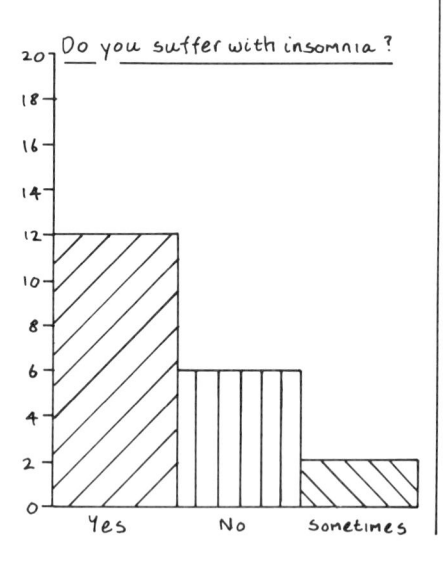

[Bar chart titled "Do you suffer with insomnia?" with y-axis from 0 to 20. Yes: 12, No: 6, Sometimes: 2]

Section C: Interpreting the survey results

Of the twenty nurses sampled 85 per cent said that they found their work stressful, with the remaining 15 per cent saying they experienced stress sometimes. I found it sad that not one nurse could say that she never suffered from career related stress.

The most common symptoms were insomnia and depression, although a greater percentage suffered from insomnia more frequently. Thirty per cent of nurses admitted to drinking and smoking regularly. This I found surprisingly high, considering that nurses are fully aware of the health risks.

After examining my data I found that there was no link between age, or even length of time worked in the department, and suffering from stress. So it seems that stress does not diminish the longer one is nursing.

However, in answer to the question, 'do you intend to stay in the Accident and Emergency Department?', 75 per cent said they had no other plans. The remaining 25 per cent were merely unsure. Incidentally, the questionnaires were answered anonymously so as to encourage genuine responses. In spite of the stressful nature of the job it is clear why nurses chose to work in this particular department. They like the excitement and variety it offers, as these comments show: 'I like the pace of work, the variety and excitement'; 'I enjoyed the exciting nature of the work as a student and came back for more'; 'I like demanding work and you certainly get it in this department'.

Section D: Conclusion

Drawing on all my research, both primary and secondary, I can confidently state that nursing is a stressful occupation. All my evidence confirms this conclusion whilst no evidence that I have collected contradicts it. The use of a variety of methods has helped me be as objective as possible. Objectivity is very important since reliable results depend on it.

The degree of stress in nursing is very high. The Registrar General's occupational mortality list places nursing near the top and my questionnaire showed that 85 per cent of nurses found their work stressful.

This project has really broadened my awareness and understanding of casualty nursing. I now have much greater sympathy for nurses and hope that if I am ever in a hospital waiting for treatment I will not be impatient or rude. I only wish that similar enquiries could be made available to the public so that we in general could become more understanding. This would reduce a major cause of stress in nursing, namely, patients constantly complaining about the delay in receiving treatment.

Section E: Appendix

I feel that my project went really well, and I enjoyed completing it as I found it informative and interesting.

I think that my research methods were, though not faultless, effective in that their combined qualities helped me to test and to prove objectively my hypothesis.

Participant observation helped a great deal, although if I was to repeat this project I would try to take part in the nurses' duties. This would give me a greater insight into their work. I would also choose to carry out my observations at two hospitals. By restricting myself to Whipps Cross I am unable to determine if this is a typical hospital.

Although my questionnaire provided many sound statistics I now feel that questions 7 and 8 should have been made into four questions as they were asking for four different pieces of information.

I would have liked to have given questionnaires to the patients as well, to provide another view, but red-tape prevented this.

The in-depth interview provided useful information, but I wish that I had had the courage to probe further. Also, taping the interview would have made writing it up easier.

Finally, I would like to have returned to the hospital to see whether any of my self-conscious feelings had disappeared, and to compare visits.

Data-response questions

1. Using Section A:
   (a) How did Kerry prepare for her role as a participant observer?
   (b) Why did Kerry find her experience in the hospital stressful?
2. Using Section B, what percentage of the sample answered yes to the question, 'do you suffer from insomnia'?
3. Using Section C, why did Kerry use confidential questionnaires?
4. Using Section D, what is one of the causes of stress experienced by nurses that the public could remove?
5. Using Section E:
   (a) Explain why the use of a variety of research methods in a study is important and valuable.
   (b) Why is it important to include in a research study a discussion of the methods used to collect information?

Discussion

What criticisms can be made of participant observation as a research method?

Research suggestion

Hypothesis: Teaching is a stressful occupation.
Method: Give a questionnaire to a representative sample of teachers. Perhaps it could be arranged for you to gain first-hand experience by actually teaching, say, a first-year class.

though it is not always easy to give these students, parents, etc., as neat labels. In various ways, Barker triangulated her research, as some would put it, by using a range of different methods which were appropriate to her research topic.

Studies using mixed methods

Source A

Researching child abuse

SOCIETY TODAY

SOCIETY TODAY IS NEW SOCIETY'S weekly termtime page, designed for A level and other sociology students.

PAT McNEILL talks to **STEVE TAYLOR** of the London School of Economics about the qualitative methods he uses to research child abuse. This is part of an occasional series of such interviews.

PAT McNEILL: What is the subject of your research?
STEVE TAYLOR: I'm researching child abuse, and in particular how various experts, such as social workers and doctors, come to "recognise" that a child has been abused or is "at risk."
PM: Is your work intended to guide social policy in this area?
ST: As a sociologist, what concerns me is that most people researching this area oversimplify the problem. They assume that there is a thing called child abuse which is relatively easy to define, that it happens, and that it is easy to identify who is being abused. For them, the only questions are about why it happens.

I think the sociologist has to say: "Before we get into those questions we must see what we mean by child abuse, what officials mean by child abuse and how we respond to what we perceive to be child abuse." Then you can say to social workers, doctors and others: "These are the theories you are implicitly working with when you define one case as child abuse and another as normal parenting. What do you think of these theories? Do you want to go back and re-examine them? Do you think you should be doing anything differently?" This type of research can help practitioners to clarify their thinking and improve the quality of their work.

PM: What research methods are you using?
ST: First, we did formal interviews with the various professional groups involved. We asked them how they defined child abuse, and how they recognised something as a case of child abuse. But sociologists should not just reproduce what people say, and you cannot conduct research purely on interviews. So, having identified some of the things professionals saw as problematic about child abuse, we did some participant observation. This meant going out with social workers on visits, going to case conferences and to court in order to see their ideas in action.

At the same time, we were able to put further questions; for example, asking social workers to explain particular decisions. We also used documentary data, such as social work files and case conference minutes.

We formed the impression during the research that social services felt under such pressure from the media, from policy guidelines and from lack of resources that they were being more defensive and were bringing more cases to court than they really wished to, or would have done a few years earlier. Official figures show that the proportion of children coming into care compulsorily has increased in the last few years. Some people suggest that this is because abuse is on the increase. Our data suggests that it can be explained by our changing response to children at risk.

At one point I played the role of a trainee social worker. The advantage of this was that I could be more sure that people weren't being extra efficient and careful for my benefit. The disadvantage was that I couldn't stop people and ask them research questions. It's not a question of a right or wrong method. You pick your method to suit the nature of the problem, and you look for interplay between methods.
PM: Is it difficult to keep your own personal values distinct from the research you are doing?
ST: If we let our personal values predominate, then we cease to be sociologists. Just recently, every politician and pundit has suddenly become an expert on child abuse. If you are on the political right, it's because of the decline in family values. If you are left of centre, it's because of bad housing, stress, and the deprivations of capitalism. If you are into feminism, it's just another example of male power.

All these views are immediate political responses, and there is an important distinction between politics and sociology. Politicians only look for evidence to confirm a pre-conceived view. Sociology, on the other hand, is about discovery. The sociologist may have pre-conceived views, but research must be structured so that there is always the chance of discovering the unexpected.

You must also keep your emotions as well as your values out of research. As a citizen, child abuse alarms me. As a social scientist, it is behaviour to be observed and analysed.

(from *New Society*, 15 January 1988)

Source B: *The Making of a Moonie*

Eileen Barker started her research on why people became members of the Unification Church in 1976. Her study was published in 1984. She used three main methods:

1 Interviews
She conducted thirty in-depth interviews with followers during 1977. Most interviews lasted between six and eight hours. All were taped.

2 Participant observation
She visited a number of Unification Centres in Britain, the USA and Scandinavia. Her role as observer went through three stages:

- a passive stage where she did very little except watch and listen – 'doing the washing up in the kitchen was always a good place for this';
- an interactive stage where she could join in conversations and learn to use the same 'social language';
- an active stage where she was able to ask awkward questions and argue.

3 Questionnaires
She obtained 380 respondents to a forty-one-page questionnaire from amongst Moonies; and 110 respondents to a thirty-six-page questionnaire

from non-Moonies, who were matched to the Moonie respondents with respect to sex, age and background. The non-Moonie respondents were used as the 'control group'. 'For the pre-coded questions the respondent would ring the most applicable of a series of possible answers; the open questions could be answered by the respondent in any way he chose . . . Two research assistants coded the response so that the information could be fed into a computer.'

She also used application lists to send questionnaires to those who had attended recruitment sessions, contacted almost a hundred sets of parents, and contacted a number of 'anti-cult' organisations.

(adapted from *The Making of a Moonie* by Eileen Barker, Basil Blackwell, 1984)

Source C: *Ante-Natal Care Re-assessed*

Between 1976 and 1984 medical sociologists were involved in assessing the old system of ante-natal care in Aberdeen and comparing it with a new system, introduced in 1980. Among the changes under scrutiny was the new arrangement whereby pregnant women had fewer visits to hospitals and more check-ups with local doctors or mid-wives. Data was collected in the following ways (figures in brackets indicate achieved numbers on whom data were collected):

1 Clinical appraisals
Scrutiny of case notes of all women who had delivered babies in Aberdeen in 1975 (1,907).
Clinical study of case notes of deliveries (1,634)

2 Observational data
Observation of consultations between pregnant women and obstetricians.

- before the innovation (380)
- after the innovation (375)

3 Questionnaire data
Questionnaires were distributed to those attending clinics asking them about the costs of coming (lost wages, transport and child-care costs) while staff noted how long their check up took.

- before the innovation (532)
- after the innovation (723)

4 Interview data
Expectant mothers were interviewed in their homes and asked about their experiences when visiting the ante-natal clinic

- before the innovation (50)
- after the innovation (232)

Open-ended interviews were also tape-recorded with obstetricians, mid-wives, general practitioners and health visitors.

(adapted from *Ante-Natal Care Re-assessed* by M. Hall, S. Macintyre and M. Porter, Aberdeen University Press, 1985)

Data-response questions

1 Using Source A:
   (a) What sort of documentary data did Steve Taylor use?
   (b) Where did he carry out participant observation?
   (c) Why did he play the role of a trainee social worker?
   (d) What does he see as the difference between politicians and sociologists?
2 Using Source B:
   (a) What was the aim of Eileen Barker's research?
   (b) Name the three research methods that she used.
   (c) What was her purpose in having a 'control group'?
   (d) Why was it important that her control group matched her sample of Moonies in respect of age, sex and background?
3 Using Source C:
   (a) List the different research methods used in the study referred to in this source.
   (b) Why was it necessary for this study to be carried out over a number of years?

Discussion

'Sociologists must keep their emotions and values out of their research.'

Research suggestion

Hypothesis: Leisure time differs more between middle- and working-class teenagers than between male and female teenagers.
Method: Use a variety of methods, such as observation, questionnaires and interviews.

Sampling

Source A: A longitudinal study

Source B: Sheer hype?

The lifetime of a generation

Neville Butler has been studying a group of 17-year-olds since they were born. His final report promises to be the most comprehensive yet on teenagers. John Cunningham reports

Few people can know more about young people than Neville Butler. His wizard info. is focused on seventeen-year-olds. Every seventeen-year-old, in fact, who was born in England, Scotland and Wales in a single week in April, 1970. He has been studying their progress at five-yearly intervals since birth, to produce the biggest report on a rising generation.

Butler's group under study numbered 15,000 when he began his investigation. Already, 3 per cent have died; 4 per cent have gone to live abroad with their families. Every year 10 per cent change their addresses, making them harder to trace. Others haven't bothered to reply. This means that the sample has shrunk to 10,000.

Butler, former Professor of Child Health at Bristol University, has been asking them to fill in lots of questions on every aspect of their lives. There are also reports by teachers, health visitors and parents. It is doubtful that a more thorough inquiry has ever been done.

Professor Butler is proud of the way the questions have been framed. To get the right tone on those about sex, for example, he got his researchers to go out with tape recorders to find out how teenagers discussed the subject among themselves – 'so that it wouldn't seem as though an old fuddy-duddy was asking them'.

Already, some glimpses are on offer about these young adults. 'They're very articulate. They tend to know what they want. They're a very caring generation, if a Right wing one,' says Butler. They're against racism, but three-quarters of them want capital punishment brought back for serious crimes, and flogging for football hooligans. Asked whether gays should be prosecuted, 40 per cent agreed fully or partly that they should. Almost 70 per cent said they should be getting sex education from their parents, rather than from teachers.

They are well clued up on Aids, so much so on the basis of their answers and essays that Butler wonders whether the government isn't targeting the wrong group in its advertising campaign, and believes that older people perhaps need more information.

There are concerns for a wide spectrum of the political and commercial lobbies. Present results indicate that the group rates terrorism and violence as more pressing problems than the arms race or environmental pollution.

'A good half of them seem to be eating chips with everything. When you are sixteen, you need a lot of carbohydrates, so we'll have to wait and see if it makes any difference by the time they are adults.' A lot of food manufacturers will be anxious about the findings; part of the survey involves respondents keeping a dietary diary in which they have to record every meal, snack, bite and drink – as well as the brand names of all processed food consumed.

(adapted from the *Guardian*, 29 December 1987)

SHERE HITE'S latest massive study, Women And Love, has been savaged with phenomenal ferocity in America. A cover story in Time magazine ripped her apart; Newsweek trashed her; a two-page investigation in the Washington Post followed. This erstwhile hottest of best selling authors has now not even found a paperback publisher for her book in America.

The argument has been entirely about her statistical methods and her personality, and scarcely at all about her message. She sent out 100,000 questionnaires to women all over the country, and the book is based on the 4,500 replies from which she draws her conclusions. From her research, she found that most women are deeply dissatisfied with their relationships with men.

The Washington Post assembled various statistical experts who dismissed her work on numerous grounds. Others said women who are prepared to fill out a lengthy 127-question form, writing essays on many answers, would be bound to have an atypical view. Did only angry and dissatisfied women reply?

She does invite such criticism by making extravagantly high claims for her sample, breaking down the answers into figures, some of which simply lack the ring of credibility — 98 per cent of women dissatisfied, 70 per cent of married women currently having affairs — which is a shame since the figures are the least important part of the book's impact.

(from the *Guardian*, 25 February 1988)

Source C: Sampling young mums

In her research for *Women Attached: The Daily Lives of Women with Young Children* (Croom Helm, 1985), Jacqueline Tivers limited her survey population to women with at least one child under the age of full-time schooling in the London Borough of Merton. She had the resources for only three weeks of interviewing and she hoped for a sample of 400.

She considered a number of methods of sampling:

- Approach women from names on the electoral register. The problem with this method is that too many would not have young children. The percentage of households without young children was as high as 96 per cent in some districts according to data from the 1971 census.
- Playgroup registers 'would obviously have biased the sample in favour of women who were more involved in outside activities'.
- Primary school lists of future pupils 'would be more likely to contain the names of children whose mothers were interested in education or those with brothers and sisters already at school'.
- Birth records would not give the addresses of those who had moved into or moved within the borough. In any case this information is classified and not easily available to researchers.
- Over 90 per cent of babies attend health clinics but access to the records of clinics in Merton was refused on the grounds of confidentiality.

The chosen method involved two stages:

- Select a stratified sample of 100 out of the 375 census enumeration districts in Merton. In other words, Tivers made sure that she included high and low social class areas.
- Four respondents were then located in each district by using a simple 'snow-balling' method. The first young mother was found by questioning residents. She was then asked where other young mothers lived. 'In some areas containing very few mothers with young children, it was necessary to knock on every door in order to obtain interviews.'

All interviews were carried out during the day-time hours on weekdays. This meant that the sample was weighted towards women who spent more time at home and, in particular, against those who were out at work full-time. In this 1977 survey 4.7 per cent of the young mums were living in households without a husband present. The 1971 census for the borough of Merton gave this figure as 5.4 per cent of the total.

Data-response questions

1. Using Source A:
   (a) What sample is Professor Butler's study based on?
   (b) How frequently has he been following up the sample in this longitudinal study?
   (c) Why has the size of his original sample declined over the years?
   (d) How did Butler try to ensure that the questions he asked were worded in order to get the information he wanted?
2. Using Source B:
   (a) What response rate did Shere Hite obtain for her 'Women and Love' survey?
   (b) How would you criticise Hite's research methods?
3. Using Source C:
   (a) Why did Jacqueline Tivers not use the electoral register to obtain her sample?
   (b) Tivers used a stratified sample. What is a 'stratified sample'?
   (c) Why did Tivers compare her sample with figures from the 1971 census?
4. What can be learned from Sources A, B and C about the problems of obtaining a representative sample?

Discussion

To what extent do your teenage friends share the attitudes and value of the young people studied by Butler?

Research suggestion

Hypothesis: Young people are well informed on the subject of Aids.
Method: After deciding upon a definition of 'young people', select a representative sample and administer a questionnaire. You could make this a comparative study by altering the hypothesis to 'Young people are better informed about Aids than older people'.

An example of a questionnaire

These questions are part of a questionnaire which was sent to all policewomen and also to a random, representative 10 per cent sample of all policemen in the 'Medshire' police force in 1983.

Please tick the appropriate boxes

1. Male ☐
   Female ☐

2. Age
   18 to 24 ☐
   25 to 34 ☐   45 to 54 ☐
   35 to 44 ☐   55 and over ☐

3. Marital status
   Single ☐   Widowed ☐
   Married ☐   Divorced ☐

4. Number of children (if any) ....

5. Rank ....

6. Length of service
   Under 2 yrs ☐   15 to 20 yrs ☐
   2 to 5 yrs ☐   20 to 25 yrs ☐
   5 to 10 yrs ☐   Over 25 yrs ☐
   10 to 15 yrs ☐

7. Qualifications when you joined the police service:

   CSE/O-Levels ☐   How many? ☐
   A-Levels ☐   How many? ☐
   OND ☐   Degree ☐
   HND ☐   None ☐
   Other (please specify) ....

34. Compared with police officers of the opposite sex, how would you assess **your own capability** in each of the following situations? (tick the response which applies to you for each task)

	Better	Same	Worse
a. General purpose motor patrol			
b. Clerical work			
c. Child abuse cases			
d. Motoring offences			
e. Foot patrol			
f. Questioning victims of rape/or indecency offences			
g. Writing reports			
h. Traffic accidents			
i. Interviewing female suspects			
j. Observation work			
k. Domestic disputes			
l. Getting information at the scene of a crime			
m. Dealing with a crowd of 4–6 male drunks on the street			
n. Juvenile offenders			
o. Threatening situations where someone has a knife			
p. Interviewing male suspects			
q. Community liaison			

35. Which of the following definitions most closely describes the way in which **you think** policewomen should be employed in the police service:

    Policewomen should take on **all** the same duties as policemen. ☐

    Policewomen should take on similar duties to policemen **except** those where violence is anticipated. ☐

    Policewomen should **not** do the same work as policemen, but should specialise in duties such as female offenders and victims, juveniles and children, and missing persons. ☐

38. Please indicate how far you agree or disagree with each of the following statements by ticking the appropriate box.

	Strongly agree	Agree	Neither agree nor disagree	Disagree	Strongly disagree	Don't know
Since integration there has been a serious loss of expertise in dealing with young people, female offenders and missing persons.						
Since integration women officers are involved in far more interesting work.						
Policemen find it difficult to accept that women should perform the same duties as they do.						
Policewomen do not have the physical strength that is required for police duties.						
Most policewomen leave the police service in order to get married and/or have a family.						

39. What proportion of your work would you **estimate** involves the possibility of physical violence:
    Less than 10% ☐
    Up to a quarter ☐
    Up to a half ☐
    More than half ☐

40. Please indicate whether you have ever been in any of the following situations during the course of your duties as a police officer:

   Been threatened verbally ☐

   Struggled, unaided, with a violent person ☐

   Been threatened by someone with a knife, gun or other weapon. ☐

   Been physically assaulted ☐

   If you have at some time been physically assaulted please answer the following questions:
   How many times have you been physically assaulted?
   Number ☐

   Did any of these assaults result in you being injured?
   Yes ☐
   No ☐

   If **yes**, for each occasion please indicate whether your injuries were minor or serious.

	Minor	Serious		Minor	Serious
1.	☐	☐	4.	☐	☐
2.	☐	☐	5.	☐	☐
3.	☐	☐			

42. Has a member of the public ever made a complaint about the way you perform your police duties?
   Yes ☐
   No ☐

   If **yes**, did this complaint result in formal investigation under the complaints procedure?
   Yes ☐
   No ☐

The following questions are for policewomen who joined the police service before integration (before 1975)

Policewomen only
If you joined the police service before integration (before 1975) please answer the following questions

43. Listed below are some of the changes, resulting from integration, which are said to affect policewomen. Please indicate (by ticking the appropriate box) how far you **agree** or **disagree** that these have affected you.

	Strongly agree	Agree	Neither agree nor disagree	Disagree	Strongly disagree	Don't know
There is a greater variety of work.						
Shifts, night duty and irregular hours disrupt personal life.						
There is more chance to specialise, for example, in the CID.						
There is more exposure to danger and violence.						
Working relationships have improved.						
Policewomen have equal status with policemen.						

(from *Policewomen and Equality* by Sandra Jones, Macmillan, 1986)

Q Data-response questions

1 Most of the above questions are 'structured' and 'closed'. What do these two terms mean?
2 Most of the above questions ask for factual information but question 35 asks about attitudes. Explain this difference.
3 From the questions and the study's title,
   (a) what do you suppose was the aim of the study?
   (b) why was it funded by the Equal Opportunities Commission?
4 Why was the questionnaire first sent to thirty officers in a pilot study?
5 What are the advantages and disadvantages of using postal questionnaires?
6 Explain the meaning of the term 'interviewer bias'.

D Discussion

'The best way to investigate sex equality in the police force would be to carry out observational research, both in police stations and on patrol with male and female officers.'

R Research suggestion

Invite your local police liaison officer to visit you for an in-depth, unstructured interview on the topic of equal opportunities for women in the police force.

This could be expanded into a project by examining official sources of documentary information concerning the recruitment, deployment and promotion of police officers and by carrying out further interviews with police officers.

2 Gender roles

Body images

Source **A**

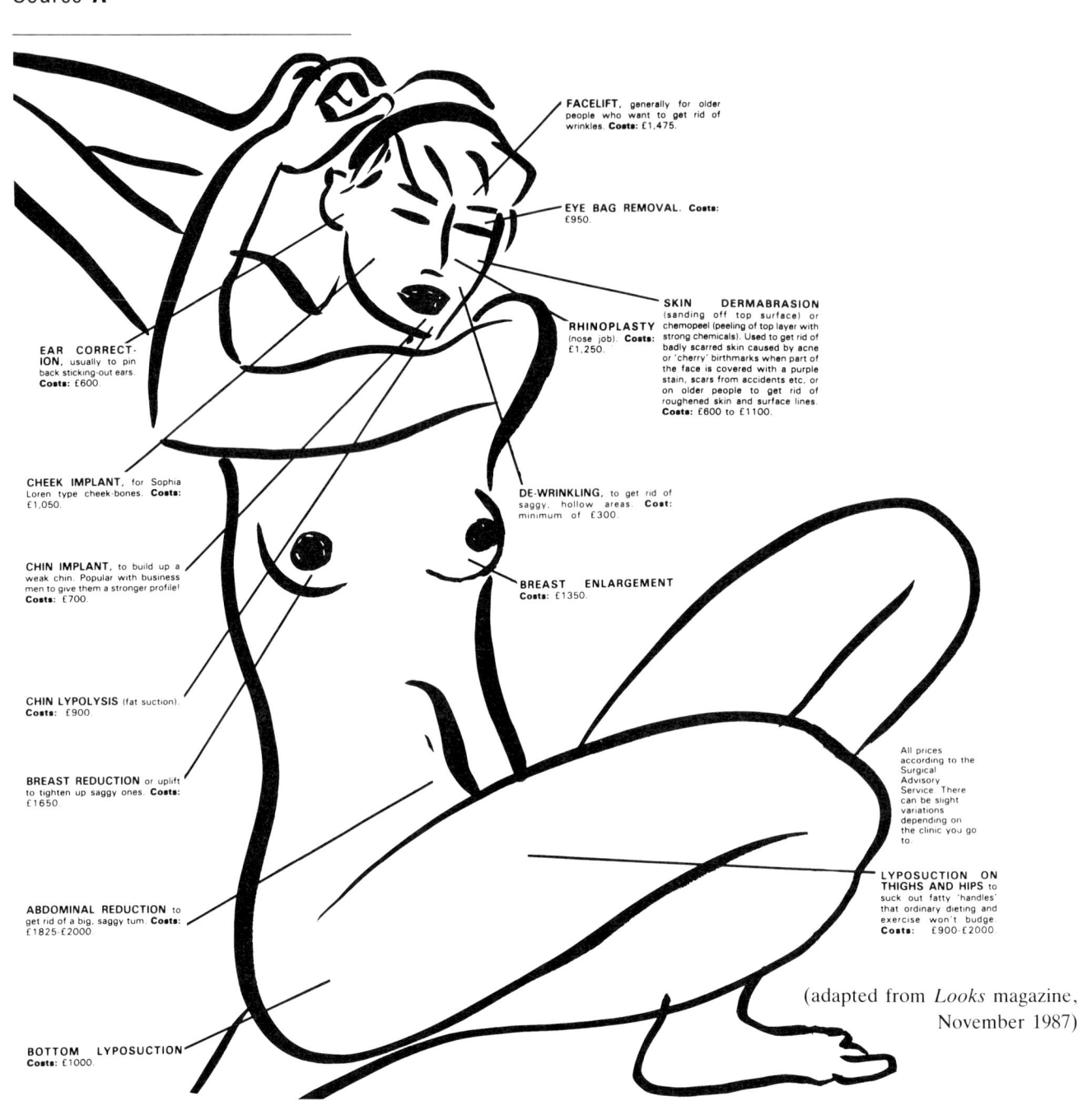

FACELIFT, generally for older people who want to get rid of wrinkles. **Costs:** £1,475.

EYE BAG REMOVAL. **Costs:** £950.

RHINOPLASTY (nose job). **Costs:** £1,250.

SKIN DERMABRASION (sanding off top surface) or chemopeel (peeling of top layer with strong chemicals). Used to get rid of badly scarred skin caused by acne or 'cherry' birthmarks when part of the face is covered with a purple stain, scars from accidents etc, or on older people to get rid of roughened skin and surface lines. **Costs:** £600 to £1100.

EAR CORRECTION, usually to pin back sticking-out ears. **Costs:** £600.

CHEEK IMPLANT, for Sophia Loren type cheek-bones. **Costs:** £1,050.

CHIN IMPLANT, to build up a weak chin. Popular with business men to give them a stronger profile! **Costs:** £700.

DE-WRINKLING, to get rid of saggy, hollow areas. **Cost:** minimum of £300.

BREAST ENLARGEMENT **Costs:** £1350.

CHIN LYPOLYSIS (fat suction). **Costs:** £900.

BREAST REDUCTION or uplift to tighten up saggy ones. **Costs:** £1650.

All prices according to the Surgical Advisory Service. There can be slight variations depending on the clinic you go to.

LYPOSUCTION ON THIGHS AND HIPS to suck out fatty 'handles' that ordinary dieting and exercise won't budge. **Costs:** £900-£2000.

ABDOMINAL REDUCTION to get rid of a big, saggy tum. **Costs:** £1825-£2000.

BOTTOM LYPOSUCTION **Costs:** £1000.

(adapted from *Looks* magazine, November 1987)

Source **B**

(from *Women in the World* by J. Seager and A. Olson, 1986)

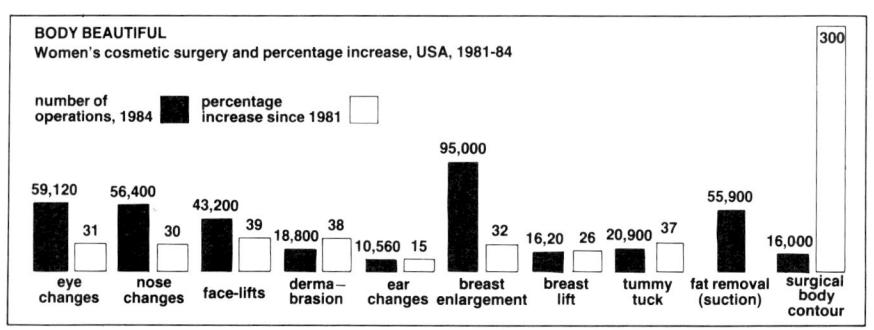

BODY BEAUTIFUL
Women's cosmetic surgery and percentage increase, USA, 1981-84

number of operations, 1984 ■ percentage increase since 1981 □

category	number	% increase
eye changes	59,120	31
nose changes	56,400	30
face-lifts	43,200	39
dermabrasion	18,800	38
ear changes	10,560	15
breast enlargement	95,000	32
breast lift	16,20	26
tummy tuck	20,900	37
fat removal (suction)	55,900	
surgical body contour	16,000	300

Gender roles

Source C

NURSES ARM THEMSELVES

NURSES who are arming themselves with scissors to fight off muggers and sex pests have been warned by police that they could end up in court.

The "angels" are terrified because an acute lack of parking spaces at Bristol's Royal Infirmary forces them to walk anything up to a mile through dark back streets from public car parks. "I always carry a pair of scissors in my hand at night," one nurse said yesterday.

(from the *Daily Mirror*, 26 Nov. 1987)

Source E: The day's glamour girl

(from the *Daily Mirror*, 18 Nov. 1988)

Source D

WHAT A PAIR! (JOAN AND HER GUY, THAT IS..)

DYNASTY queen Joan Collins made up a delightful pair at a glittering Hollywood ball. With her was her favourite man, Bungalow Bill Wiggins, who escaped being drawn into the picture. Joan flew into London yesterday for another star-studded ball — this time in aid of leukaemia research.

FRONT LINE: Joan presents an impressive twosome at the Hollywood ball
ESCORT: Bill

Q Data-response questions

1. What is the most popular type of women's cosmetic surgery in the USA?
2. Why has a man's body not been used for the illustration in Source A?
3. Women's bodies are shown for different purposes in Sources A, D and E. Identify these different purposes.
4. What effect do you think such images of women have
   (a) on the attitudes of men to women?
   (b) on the attitudes of women to themselves?

D Discussion

Sources C, D and E all come from the *Daily Mirror*. 'A rapist treats his victim as an object.' Is the *Daily Mirror* creating potential rapists by its images of women?

R Research suggestion

Hypothesis: Males are less dissatisfied with their bodies than females.
Method: Write a short questionnaire on this issue for a sample of males and females. Questions could include: 'Do you ever go on a diet?' 'If you could afford it, would you seriously consider any of the sorts of plastic surgery shown in Source A?'

Gender roles

Socialisation

Source A: Mickey Rourke

(from *Time Out*, 11–18 Nov. 1987)

Source B: Patsy Kensit

(from *Mizz*, Summer Special, 1988)

Source C: 'Men and Men'

Boys grow up to be wary of each other. We are taught to compete with one another in school, and to struggle to prove ourselves outside it, on the street, the playground and the sports field. Later we fight for status over sexual reputation, or money, or physical strength, or technical know-how. We fear to admit to our weaknesses to one another, to admit our failures, our vulnerability, and we fear being called a cissy, a wet or a softie. We fear humiliation, or exclusion, or ultimately, the violence of other boys if we fail to conform.

This mask fits in with the kinds of roles we are expected to play when we come to start work where, at its most extreme, we are expected simply to be extensions of our machines, or of our job descriptions, and where our fear of other men makes us effective wielders and obeyers of authority, in a system that is based on top-down discipline rather than co-operation. At its most extreme, scientists and engineers and politicians prove their manhood by perfecting ever more destructive weapons systems to assure mutual destruction to the nth degree, while the simplest basic problems of mankind – food, clean air, housing – attract little comparable energy or investment.

Male chumminess often expresses men's deep desire for genuine friendship with other men. But at work this chumminess occurs in a context which is designed to put men in competition with one another. The desire for friendship is all too often confused with an alliance *against* any influence which might threaten male superiority and pride – women, gay men, lesbians, people of other races and colours, short men, fat men, disabled people . . . The style of this contradiction between desire and outside pressure often emerges as piss-taking, a contact that is at once a reaching out and a keeping at bay.

(adapted from 'About Men' by Paul Morrison and Tony Eardley, in *The English Curriculum: Gender – Material for Discussion*, ILEA English Centre, 1985)

Q Data-response questions

1 What images of masculinity and femininity are expressed by Sources A and B?
2 Using Source C:
   (a) Why do boys grow up to be wary of each other?
   (b) Why are boys afraid to admit to failures and to being sensitive?
   (c) Boys are expected to acquire certain qualities. How do these qualities prepare them for the jobs which they are likely to do?
   (d) Explain why men are inclined to make fun of women and of males who are different from themselves.

D Discussion

How far do you agree with the points made in Source C?

R Research suggestion

Hypothesis: Magazines for teenage girls are mainly concerned with 'getting your man' while magazines for teenage boys encourage interests such as computers and sport.
Method: Analyse and compare the contents of a sample of magazines for teenagers.

Women in restaurants

Source A: 'Sexist practices at the table' by Nigella Lawson

I can go into a restaurant with a man, tell the person at the door that I've booked a table, give the name the table's booked under, and still be sure that the waiter will ask him whether we'd like a drink, give him the wine list and expect him to order. . . .

Going to a restaurant with another woman, or 'alone' as men with telling unselfconsciousness tend to see it (as in : 'Why are you two girls eating here all alone?') poses another set of problems. . . . If I go out for dinner with another woman, which I frequently do, it is an act of choice, not desperation. I certainly don't want to be chatted up by the waiters.

(from *The Spectator*, 14 November 1987)

Source B: Common examples of the way in which women handle men's feelings

Looking around the tables, we were struck by just how many women were smiling at men and how few men were smiling at women in return . . . We continued to observe and to listen, to note and to speculate; we had a data-gathering field day in that restaurant. We watched two women who appeared to be quite content chatting to each other. They were approached by a man who interrupted their conversation. And they smiled. After a few 'polite' exchanges, he withdrew . . . He had come to request the pleasure of their company and it had been rather awkward getting him to take no for an answer.

What exactly did he say, we asked, trying to establish why the women had smiled at the man. While it could have been a source of amusement that he had said, 'As you two are alone, why don't you join my friend and me', we realised that the women did not see anything funny in the man describing them as being 'alone'. There was nothing funny in what he had said that warranted a smile as far as they were concerned.

'We didn't want to join him and his friend,' she explained. 'But we didn't want him to feel badly about it. I don't think he felt rejected.'

(from *Reflecting Men: at twice their natural size* by S. Cline and D. Spender, André Deutsch, 1987)

Q Data-response questions

1 What is odd about the question 'Why are you two girls eating here all alone?'
2 Cline and Spender claim that body posture and smiling are part of the elaborate ritual by which women boost men and 'reflect men at twice their natural size'. What evidence do they offer in Source B?

D Discussion

1 Do you agree with Cline and Spender that women continually
   • come to the rescue of men who are being embarrassing, rude or stupid;
   • protect men, placate men, prop up men's pride;
   • use numerous ploys to place men at the centre of attention and to reassure them of their significance?
2 What are the ways in which women put down men?

R Research suggestion

Hypothesis: Our culture requires women to smile (continually) at men.
Method: Female students could try to test the results of the week long smile boycott which was carried out by New York receptionists. As well as immediate, and interminable, queries of 'What's wrong with you?', some men got wildly abusive and accused the receptionists of deliberately 'ruining the day'.

Gender and schooling

Ruler wanging in mixed classrooms

A sample observation sheet — 5 MINUTE TICK SHEET

TAPPING					
FEET SHUFFLING					
CHEWING					
RULER WANGING					
HAND UP					
CALLING OUT					
TOPIC TALK					
NON TOPIC TALK					
LISTENING TO T					
LISTENING TO P					
READING					
READING ALOUD					
WRITING					
CHAIR ROCKING					
BAG ON TABLE					
KNOCKING CHAIRS					
SHOVE HA'PENNY					
MOCK FIGHT					
SHARING IDEAS					
MISUSING MATERIAL					
MAKE-UP					
BRUSHING HAIR					
STARING INTO SPACE					
OUT OF SEAT					
SHOWING WORK T					
SHOWING WORK P					

When Margaret Sandra observed English lessons in a South London comprehensive school she found that certain activities could be identified with one sex or the other. Here are some of them:

Girls
hand up
chewing
reading
make up
brushing hair
showing work to teacher

Boys
calling out
pencil tapping
chair rocking
bag on table
shove ha'penny
misusing materials

Girls controlled their environment by controlling themselves. Boys controlled the environment by controlling others: teachers, girls and other boys.

Only a relatively small proportion of boys cause the disruption. Their techniques are not consciously thought out but they serve a purpose: they distract the teacher and themselves from what underpins their activities – insecurity and fear of failure. I base this on my observation that this core of boys consistently produced less writing than the girls and spent less time on topic-centred talk.

The more I consider the world these boys inhabit the more I recognise how narrow it is. The masculine role is to be an authority in some way, on football, cars, fishing and now computers. Disrupting an English lesson by not having a pen or tripping a neighbour as he/she walks past reduces the amount of time needed to explore feelings, yours and theirs.

Eighteen thousand more boys than girls left school in 1983 with no qualification in English. Ten thousand more girls than boys achieved pass grades in O-level English or equivalent. The figures must be a cause for concern, both in terms of boys' underachievement and the underestimation of girls. Ruler wanging and applying make-up are clearly not the cause of such differences in pupil performance and teacher expectation but they are signs of a wider set of sex-role expectations which invade the classroom.

(adapted from 'Ruler Wanging and Other Noises' by Margaret Sandra, in *The English Curriculum: Gender – Material for Discussion*, ILEA English Centre, 1985)

Data-response questions

1. What sex differences were there in the English results in 1983?
2. Which female activities show that sex-role stereotypes 'invade the classroom'?
3. How did boys control the environment?
4. Why, according to the writer, did boys disrupt their English lessons?

Discussion

1. Why do many girls make more progress in single-sex rather than co-educational schools?
2. What are the disadvantages of single-sex schooling?

Research suggestion

Hypothesis: Boys and girls act differently in the classroom.
Method: Record observations on Margaret Sandra's checklist.

Source A: Are boys more important than girls in schools?

Teachers are very often unaware of the way they allocate their time. If asked whether they give more attention to one sex than the other, it is common for them to strongly protest that they do *not*. They claim that they treat both sexes equally but tapes of their lessons show that over two-thirds of their time is spent with the boys.

In Michelle Stanworth's study of schooling in Cambridge, she asked students: 'Who receives the most attention in class?' and 'What sort of attention do they get?' The students provided the following data:

- four boys joined in classroom discussions for every one girl;
- teachers were twice as likely to ask boys questions;
- they were three times more likely to praise and encourage boys.

Both the boys and the girls stated that teachers

- are more concerned about boys;
- consider boys to be more capable;
- enjoy teaching boys more.

From the pupils' point of view there is agreement that teachers consider male students to be more important. This adds to the confidence of the boys (who go on to say more and demand more attention) and undermines the confidence of the girls (who react by saying less and attracting less attention).

I and many others have deliberately tried to give girls a fair share of our teaching time. When we think we have shown favouritism to the girls and been unfair on the boys, tapes in fact show that girls have had less than 35 per cent of our attention.

(adapted from 'Invisible Women' by Dale Spender, in *The English Curriculum: Gender – Material for Discussion*, ILEA English Centre, 1985)

Source B: Do girls learn to become helpless?

Carol Dweck found the following pattern of classroom interaction in Chicago:

Teachers usually praised
boys for   good pieces of work
girls for   good behaviour
Teachers usually told off
boys for   bad behaviour
girls for   bad pieces of work

From this boys learned that bad work was due to misbehaviour and lack of effort. But girls learned that poor work must be due to some failing in their ability. They learned to feel helpless and inadequate. They lost confidence in their academic ability.

In an experiment, Dweck asked teachers to try out both patterns on both girls as well as boys. The results were that

- all pupils gained in confidence if they were only told off for behaviour and only praised for the standard of their work;
- both girls and boys who were only told off for poor work and were only praised for good behaviour lost confidence.

(adapted from 'Why Girls Don't Do Science' by Alison Kelly, *New Scientist*, 20 May 1982)

Q **Data-response questions**

1. How did Michelle Stanworth collect her data?
2. How has Spender indicated that teachers with mixed classes tend to give two-thirds of their time to boys?
3. What happened when she actively tried to give girls a fair deal?
4. Girls are largely 'invisible' and boys receive more attention. What reasons are suggested for this?

D **Discussion**

'Girls tend to leave school with a low opinion of their real ability.'

R **Research suggestion**

Hypothesis: Girls receive less encouragement than boys to pursue educational qualifications and to pursue challenging careers (but this situation is gradually changing).
Method: Interview adult male and female relatives and compare their experiences with those of friends at school or college. Ask about options choice, careers guidance and the attitudes of teachers.

Women and work

Source A: Sex bias in banks

Bank alters policy on recruitment after sex bias complaint

By John Spicer, Employment Affairs Correspondent

Barclays Bank has changed its recruitment policy to ensure girls and boys have equal opportunities for promotion, in response to moves by the Equal Opportunities Commission.

The commission received a complaint from a headmaster in 1983 that his local branch of Barclays appeared to be recruiting boys and girls for different levels of work.

An inquiry by the commission revealed that Barclays recruited mainly boys with A levels, with the expectation that they would become managers.

Girl school leavers were recruited predominantly with O levels for routine clerical jobs.

The commission also found that girls appeared to be seen as short-term recruits with different career patterns from boys.

The bank offered to implement changes and the commission agreed to defer its inquiry.

A legal agreement was signed setting out all the changes proposed by Barclays.

The bank has subsequently introduced a new recruitment policy; an equal opportunity guide; training for recruitment staff to prevent discrimination and a monitoring scheme to ensure equal opportunity between the sexes.

The bank also agreed to provide the commission with statistics on recruitment for four years.

The agreeement is in its second year and the commission has said it is satisfied with the progress that has been made.

The original criticism caused particular concern because almost one million women are employed in the banking and finance sector of industry.

It has been estimated they form 60 per cent of the total employees in the four main clearing banks.

These figures mean that about 10 per cent of all women in paid employment in Britain work in banking and finance.

The banks still employ women almost exclusively in lower clerical grades and few have been promoted to management.

The commission's statistics show that in spite of the complaint, Barclays has the best record of the most well-known high street banks in promoting women into management positions.

Earlier last month Barclays attracted criticism when it withdrew the offer of a job to a girl because she was too fat.

Two similar cases involving the bank and female recruits have subsequently come to light.

In the original case, Miss Liza Costas-Paraskevas, aged 16, of Stamford Hill, north London, was told she would be reconsidered for employment if she slimmed down from 13st 7lbs to an "acceptable" 10st 12lbs.

The 5ft 4ins schoolgirl applied to the bank for a job while waiting the results of eight O levels and was told it was hers provided the results of a routine medical examination were satisfactory.

Later Mr Don Avis, a Barclay's personnel assistant, wrote to Miss Costas-Paraskevas saying the bank's doctor had reported she was overweight and could not be accepted on the bank staff.

The bank's decision was criticized by the banking workers' union, the Confederation of British Industry and the Institute of Directors.

Barclays said it was company policy for the doctor to advise on the suitability of recruits on medical grounds and his ruling was always accepted.

PERCENTAGE OF WOMEN MANAGERS

	1984	1986
MIDLAND	1.5%	2.7%
NATWEST	1.7%	1.8%
LLOYDS	2.0%	2.8%
BARCLAYS	3.5%	4.3%

(from *The Times*, 1 September 1987)

Source B: Working mothers, Great Britain, 1982

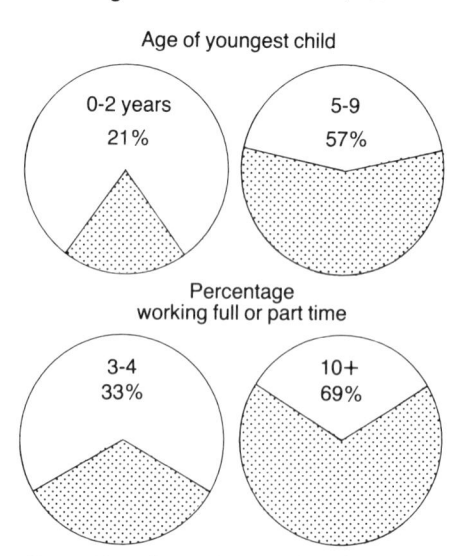

Working mothers Great Britain, 1982

Age of youngest child

- 0-2 years: 21%
- 5-9 years: 57%
- 3-4: 33%
- 10+: 69%

Percentage working full or part time

(from *New Society's* 'Database')

Source C: 'My wife doesn't work'

(from 'I want to write it down', *Writing by Women in Peckham*, 1980)

Gender roles

Source D: Education and day care of children under five in the UK

Children under five in schools		1986	1966
Public sector schools:			
nursery schools	– all day	19,000	26,000
	– part day	77,000	9,000
primary schools	– all day	306,000	220,000
	– part day	228,000	–
Private schools	– all day	20,000	21,000
	– part day	15,000	2,000
Special schools	– all day	4,000	2,000
	– part day	2,000	–

(as a percentage of all three- and four-year olds: 47%)

Day care places	1986	1966
Local authority day nurseries	33,000	21,000
Local authority playgroups	5,000	
Registered nurseries	29,000	75,000
Registered playgroups	473,000	
Registered childminders	157,000	32,000

(from *Social Trends*, HMSO, 1988)

Data-response questions

1 Using Source A:
   (a) What is the evidence that Barclays has a better reputation than other banks for promoting women?
   (b) What evidence is there that physical appearance is important for a woman?
2 Using Source B, what proportion of mothers with children under three go out to work?
3 Using Source C:
   (a) Why is the source entitled 'My wife doesn't work'?
   (b) What is common to most of the mother's activities shown?
   (c) Give an estimate of the amount of time spent on domestic work and the amount of time which the mother has for free time.
4 According to Source D, what are the most widespread forms of all-day provision for under-fives? (Can you think of any other forms of provision?)

Discussion

What sort of provision is needed for the care of children under five of mothers who wish to return to full-time work?

Research suggestion

Hypothesis: Provision for the care of under-fives has improved over the last twenty years but it is still not adequate. Many mothers of young children are prevented from returning to work by the lack of 'places' for their children.

Method Study Sources B and D and interview mothers of young children.

Gender roles

Feminism and the demands of the women's movement

- Feminism is the belief that a woman ought to be free to decide for herself how she would like to conduct her life.

- Feminism is the belief that women together could change the patriarchal ways of life that permeate our society.

- Feminism is the belief that patriarchy (male dominance) is responsible for wars, violence, rape, oppression and racism.

- Feminism is the belief that every woman has the right to define, control, and enjoy her own sexuality.

The women's movement demands:
1 Equal pay for equal work.
2 Equal education and job opportunities.
3 Free contraception and abortion on demand.
4 Free twenty-four-hour community controlled childcare.
5 Legal and financial independence for women.
6 An end to discrimination against lesbians.
7 Freedom for all women from intimidation by the threat or use of male violence. An end to laws, assumptions and institutions that perpetuate male dominance and men's aggression towards women.

(from the 15th Birthday Editorial of *Spare Rib* magazine, July 1987)

Discussion

1 Which of the demands of the women's movement are the most important and which would be the most difficult to achieve in Britain?
2 Do you agree that patriarchy is to blame for 'wars, violence, rape, oppression and racism'?

Quiz about working women (answers on p. 112)

QUIZ ABOUT WORKING WOMEN (answers on p 112)

1 In 1851 what proportion of married women were in paid employment in England?
(a) 10 per cent   (b) 25 per cent   (c) 40 per cent

2 In 1911, 9.6 per cent of married women were in the labour force. By 1977 the figure had:
(a) stayed the same   (b) doubled   (c) trebled   (d) increased five times

3 True or false? Today almost the same proportion of women in the labour force as men have responsibility for dependent children.

4 What proprtion of working mothers work part time?
(a) 20 per cent   (b) 40 per cent   (c) 60 per cent   (d) 70 per cent

5 In 1851 what was the largest occupation for women?
(a) work in textiles factories and mills   (b) clerical work
(c) agricultural work   (d) domestic service

6 True or false? There were proportionately fewer women employed in skilled occupations in 1971 than there were in 1911.

7 In which of the following industries do women constitute over 50 per cent of the labour force?
(a) mining
(b) metal manufacture
(c) textiles
(d) clothing and footwear
(e) transport and communications
(f) distributive trades
(g) professional and scientific services (e.g. education, health)
(h) miscellaneous services

8 True or false? Over 50 per cent of female manual workers work in personal service occupations (e.g. catering, cleaning, hairdressing).

9 What proportion of the clerical labour force is female?
(a) 40 per cent   (b) 60 per cent   (c) 75 per cent

10 How many homeworkers are there in the UK now? (Homeworkers are people who work at home for money but not under the management of the person who pays them. Common examples of homework are childminding, assembling electrical components, typing, sewing.)
(a) 100 000   (b) 500 000   (c) 1 million   (d) unknown

11 What proportion of managers are women?
(a) less than 15 per cent   (b) 25 per cent   (c) 40 per cent

12 True or false? The rate of increase in trade-union membership among women was five times as great as the rate of increase among men between 1966 and 1976.

13 True or false? Over 1 million women were unemployed in 1981?

14 On average, women's hourly earnings are what percentage of men's hourly earnings:
(a) 50 per cent   (b) 60 per cent   (c) 75 per cent   (d) 85 per cent

15 In 1979, 8.5 million men were in occupational pensions schemes. What number of women were in occupational pension schemes?
(a) 1 million   (b) 3 million   (c) 5 million   (d) 7 million

---

(from 'The Changing Experience of Women' by V. Beechey, in *The Changing Experience of Women, Unit 12: Economic Dependence and the State* by S. Himmelweit, Open University Press, 1983)

3 Youth and old age

Rites of Passage

Rites of Passage

Cross fingers and hope for the best – that's what most parents in the West do when their children approach adolescence. But some societies have traditions which instruct both children and parents on how to cope with the crisis.

The moment of separation from childhood can feel intensely lonely. You're out there on your own. But Jewish tradition takes care of the fear by surrounding the bar mitzvah boy with family and friends at the crucial moment.

THE *bar mitzvah* is a rite of passage which is as much a psychological milestone in the life of the parents as of the child. A boy becomes a *bar mitzvah*, literally 'a son of the laws' on his thirteenth birthday. So 'social puberty' reflects the community's general expectation of biological puberty, rather than its attainment by a particular child. It means that a boy has entered the adult Jewish community; has become a man, ready to fulfil the commandments gleaned from the Talmud, the book that codifies ancient Jewish laws and traditions.

In what was a patriarchal religion, girls were not given the same public recognition of their transition to adulthood. In recent decades that has changed. Many girls now participate in a parallel ceremony at the age of 12, called a *bat mitzvah* (*bat* means 'daughter').

The preparation for *bar mitzvah* is arduous. The child's programme of study differs from synagogue to synagogue but can last as long as two to three years, and includes Jewish history, religious ritual and classes in Hebrew, the ancient language of Judaism. The *bar mitzvah* candidate must become fluent enough to read and understand the basics of the language. And he must commit to memory the portion of the Torah (the Jewish Holy Book) that he is assigned to read on his *bar mitzvah* day.

These readings are the subject of a great deal of study and thought. The child discusses their meaning not only with his Rabbi but with other adult family members and friends and is encouraged to think about their significance in relation to his own life. So the ceremony is not, as it may seem to a cynical onlooker, empty rote-learning; it is a space created for the boy and his care-givers to explore their understanding of the soon-to-be adult's impending responsibilities.

So the social impact of the *bar mitzvah* is profound. It draws into consciousness a clear demarcation line between childhood and adulthood but even as he takes that first perilous step out of childhood, the teenager sees himself surrounded by a willing display of support and love. And at the very moment of separation into individual responsibility, the *bar mitzvah* links the boy with his history and roots.

The thirteenth birthday – a turning-point.

Recently in North America there has been criticism that some *bar mitzvahs* have degenerated into a crass display of wealth, with the religious and social meaning of the event buried under piles of gifts. But there are still many Jews who see the *bar mitzvah* as a way of enforcing their own and their children's pride and confidence in themselves and their heritage.

Says one mother in Canada who recently experienced the bustle, preparation and exhilaration of her son's *bar mitzvah*: 'Every part of his world – his parents, extended family, peers, teachers, friends – gave him approval at precisely the time when kids are most confused. It was a way for all the pieces of his life to come together, at a time of celebration. It may not have changed him consciously but I think it gave him a tremendous amount of self-confidence at a time of life when a lot of kids just fall apart.' ■

(from *New Internationalist*, August 1984)

D Discussion

1 'A British child's first assembly, in his/her new uniform at secondary school is a sort of initiation ritual. It is a social landmark signifying an important change in status: one is no longer just "a primary school kid".' From your own experience, would you agree with this statement?

2 'Adolescence is inevitably a time of crisis.'

Changing childhood and youth

Source **A:** Childhood in 1937 and 1987

The enormous gulf between youngsters in 1937 — and 50 years on

Bored Kid on Easy St

Labels on image:
- PHILIPS RADIO-CASSETTE £60
- SHARK T-SHIRT £15
- CAP 2s (10p)
- HOME-MADE CATAPULT
- BLAZER 15s 6d (77½p)
- DESIGNER JEANS £25
- ADIDAS SOCKS £5
- HI-TEC TRAINERS £25
- SKATEBOARD £45
- BOOTS 2s 6d (12½p)
- SOCKS 6d (2½p)
- SHIRT 1s 6d (7½p)
- SHORTS 4s 9d (23⅓p)

ANOTHER world . . . a 'street cred' look for the present Milky Bar Kid, David King, 12, and plain togs for his brother Steven, 11, stepping back into 1937. A father footing the bills then earned around thirty shillings (£1.50) a week, compared with £200 now.

CHILDREN of today are spoilt, indisciplined . . . and bored, says a survey.

They live in a world of computer games, new clothes and personal stereos, and expect to 'get away with anything'.

But despite being surrounded by material goods their grandparents could only have dreamt of, they are not satisfied the survey reveals.

The survey contrasting children's lifestyles now and 50 years ago, published in Woman magazine today was carried out to mark the launch of the Nestles Milky Bar in 1937.

Research psychologist Sue Keane interviewed 50 ten-year-olds, plus an equal number of 60-year-olds who were asked to recall life when they themselves were ten.

In 1937 most homes were rented, and lacked inside lavatories, bathrooms, electricity and hot water.

Children generally had only three sets of clothes — for church, school and play — and many were home-made or hand-me-downs.

Fear

They rose at about 6 am, had porridge for breafast and then walked to school, returning home for lunch. Leisure time usually revolved around games with conkers, tops, hoops and marbles and they were usualy in bed by 7.30 pm.

Youngsters today live in relative luxury, in homes where televisions, freezers and microwaves are a part of everyday life. They often get up as late as 8.30 am, skip breakfast and are driven to school where they have lunch. When they get home in the evening they play computer games or watch television and many go to bed as late as 10.30pm.

The gulf between attitudes of children today and 50 years ago is as wide as the gap between their lifestyles according to the survey.

By SUZANNE O'SHEA

In 1937 children respected — even feared — parents, teachers, policemen and relatives. If anyone reprimanded a child they would tell their parents, who administered a second punishment at home with a belt or a strop used for sharpening razors.

Nowadays punishment — usually being forced to do lines at school or being sent to the room at home — has little effect on children, whose parents now often complain if they are disciplined by the teachers.

In 1937 — when the average weekly wage was the equivalent of £1.50 — no one had enough money to save and children were aware of their families' poverty.

They earned pennies running errands or returning empty bottles and spent the money immediately in case it was taken away from them — usually buying comics or sweets, which they sucked instead of chewed to make them last.

Today fathers earn an average £200 a week and their children have building society or bank accounts in which they save birthday, Christmas and pocket money for large items such as bicycles, cassette players and televisions.

Many youngsters enjoy buying clothes to add to their already bulging wardrobes of ready-made, casual outfits, and they spend an average £3-a-week on sweets, crisps and canned drinks.

School 50 years ago, with its emphasis on the Three Rs, was either liked or loathed by children. Now it is widely regarded as boring, with computer lessons, free activity periods and playtime being listed as the most popular aspects of school life.

Nostalgia

But although children in 1937 never dreamed of foreign holidays — a commonplace event for modern children — they were also a world away from sexual attacks on children, heavy traffic, vandalism or having to lock their homes because of burglars.

And most of the 60-year-olds interviewed belived their childhoods were happier than those today.

Interviewer Mrs Keane said the viewpoints of the 60 year olds may have been coloured by nostalgia. But she thought they 'reflected fairly reasonably what they felt as children.'

(from the *Daily Mail*, 31 August 1987)

Youth and old age

Source B: The emergence of youth in the 1950s

Teddy Boys in the 1950s

Mods in the 1960s

The 1950s saw the emergence of a newly identifiable group of consumers – the young. Teenagers became an identifiable group for the first time, and acquired a high status in society, judging from attempts to appeal to them. A character in Colin MacInnes's novel, *Absolute Beginners* (1959), says of his elder brother, Vernon: 'He's one of the generations that grew up before teenagers existed . . . in poor Vernon's era . . . there just weren't any: can you believe it? . . . In those days, it seems, you were just an overgrown boy, or an undergrown man, life didn't seem to cater for anything else in between.'

A number of factors accounted for the change

1 With the expansion of welfare services and with better housing and better feeding, children matured physically at an earlier age.

2 A number of other trends – such as the raising of the school-leaving age and the greater proportion of children staying on at school – meant that more and more of these physically adult young people were remaining dependent on their parents, and were legally and politically under age. (The age of voting was not reduced to eighteen until 1970.)

3 The increasing spending power of the young marked them out as an identifiable market. In 1959 teenagers had £830 million to spend, of which the largest portion went on records. Their spending controlled over 40 per cent of the record market.

The Teddy Boys were the first of the identifiable youth factions (the name first appeared in print in March 1954) to be followed in the 1960s by the Mods, whose taste ran to all things Italian (from sharp suits and smart shoes to Vespa and Lambretta motor scooters).

(adapted from *An Economic and Social History of Britain 1760–1970* by T. May, Longman 1987)

Q Data-response questions

1 Using Source A:
   (a) How was the research about childhood in 1987 conducted?
   (b) How was the research about childhood in 1937 conducted?
   (c) Compare the leisure activities of ten-year-olds in 1937 and 1987.
   (d) Does the sample used appear to represent a cross-section of children today? If not, why not?
   (e) Do you think a fair description of modern ten-year-olds is given in this source?

2 From Source B, why is it suggested that a distinct period between childhood and adulthood emerged during the 1950s? Give three reasons.

D Discussion

'Adults tend to view their own childhoods through rose-tinted spectacles. Childhood memories provide exaggerated and unreliable evidence about the past.' What other sources can we use to learn about the recent past besides old people's memories?

R Research suggestion

Hypothesis: The most popular and unpopular aspects of school life are the same for today's pupils as for pupils fifty years ago.
Method: Interview one or two grandparents or pensioners about their schooldays and compare their views with the views of a group of your friends.

British youth cults

Source A: British youth subculture from the 1950s to the 1970s

British youth cults can be seen as responding to changing influences in society. The following chart is adapted from ideas in *Comparative Youth Culture* by Michael Brake (Routledge & Kegan Paul, 1985).

1 Teddy boys: late 1950s, working class
2 Beatniks: 1950s, middle class
3 Rockers: 1960s, working class
4 Mods: 1960s, working class
5 Skinheads: early 1970s, working class.
6 Hippies: late 1960s, middle class
7 Punks: mid 1970s, working and middle class
8 Rastas: 1970s, West Indians.

Responding positively to:	*Responding negatively to:*
A Anarchist do-it-yourself approach to bands, fashion, 'fanzines' and squatting.	Youth unemployment, youth homelessness, racism, the Queen's Silver Jubilee Year celebrations.
B 'Do your own thing' alternative lifestyles, vegetarianism, save-the-planet, get-your-head-together (e.g. Eastern mysticism).	Universities as sausage machines, the conformity of the rat race, the Vietnam war, sexual repression, racism.
C Cool, sophisticated, smart fashions of modern, upwardly mobile, officeboy in the City.	Traditional working-class ideas of work, fashion and masculinity.
D US beat novelists (e.g. Kerouac) and beat poets (e.g. Ginsberg), 'bohemian' lifestyle (e.g. hitch-hiking), jazz and folk music.	Conscription to national service, nuclear weapons, smart jobs in offices.
E Marcus Garvey's 1929 claim that Emperor Haile Selassie of Ethiopia is Jah, Ras Tafari, the living god, Lion of Judah.	'Babylon': the white agents of social control – e.g. police, teachers, employers.
F Affluence, US rock 'n' roll, fashions of the Edwardian dandy and image of Mississippi gambler.	Drabness of post-war, 'ration book Britain'; other gangs (e.g. West Indian immigrants in Notting Hill).
G Traditional boot-and-braces values of aggressive loyalty to local football team and patriotism.	Effeminate Mods and Hippies, destruction of traditional working-class jobs and communities, immigrants.
H Traditional butch masculinity, violent 'wild one' outlaw image of biker gangs (e.g. Hell's Angels).	Effeminate Mods, authority, domesticity of home life.

Q Data-response question

From Source A, match the list of eight different youth cults (1 to 8) with the list of eight characteristics (A to H). (The answers to this exercise are on p. 112.)

Youth and old age

Source B: Brutal Attack on stage at the Blood and Honour Club

(from *New Society*, 5 February 1988)

Source C: A Saturday night out at the Blood and Honour Club

In the large desolate backroom of a South London pub No Remorse are belting hell out of their instruments to an audience of about 500 British skins and 50 assorted European fascists. Around the sides of the room are little makeshift stalls selling Skrewdriver albums, fascist mags, sew-on swastikas and 'Adolf Hitler Was Right' T-shirts.

The band leader whips the audience up shouting 'Hitler and the six million Jews . . . It's all a load of shit.' The keenies at the front answer with Heil Hitler salutes.

According to *Searchlight*, the antifascist magazine: 'In the last three years, the new National Front have tried to create a street fighting force. To this end they targeted the former British Movement skinheads and the followers of Skrewdriver. Their intention was to set up a group that appeared unconnected with the NF leadership but in reality could have its strings pulled by them. They would be used for street destabilisation, fighting at sports events and keeping up racial attacks.'

Ian Stuart, the leader of Skrewdriver, recently spent a year in prison for assaulting a Nigerian at Kings Cross station. He is a self-avowed nazi who has forged strong ties with European right-wing extremists.

The Skrewdriver skins can be friendly and even eager to please to a straight white person. The ailment is not so much an undeveloped heart as an undeveloped head. Most of the skins are 16 or 17. They drink lager top and have not entirely outgrown glue. Skrewdriver simply exploit their political ignorance and latent racism.

(adapted from 'Little skins talking tall' by Amanda Mitchinson in *New Society*, 5 February 1988)

Q Data-response questions

1 Using Source B, what evidence does the picture give of the political viewpoints of the bands and their fans at the Blood and Honour Club?
2 Using Source C:
   (a) What is *Searchlight*?
   (b) According to *Searchlight*, which political party is exploiting the fans of Skrewdriver?
   (c) What sort of people are most likely to suffer as a result of the propaganda of bands like No Remorse, Brutal Attack and Skrewdriver?
   (d) Why is it ironic that the skins have scars, tattoos and shaved convict heads like the victims of the Auschwitz and Dachau death camps?

D Discussion

'Youth subcultures in Britain are best explained in terms of social class.'

R Research suggestion

In 1988, Jerry Dammers was one of the main organisers of Artists Against Apartheid's Nelson Mandela Birthday rock concert at Wembley. In the second half of the 1970s Dammers had been in a 'two-tone' band called the Specials and had helped to organise 'Rock against Racism' events.

In recent years, rock musicians have also supported charity events highlighting issues such as world hunger, discrimination against gays and Amnesty International's work for political prisoners.

Hypothesis: Bands and stars have had an increasing political impact on the young.

Method: Interview a cross-section of young people and a sample of adults who were teenagers in the 1970s. Have they been influenced by the politics in rock music? If so, in what ways?

Youth cults – a crazy phase?

Source **A**

Stories that show there's more to today's youth than meets the eye

The punk who joined the Guards

THE PUNK: Jason as he was

LOUNGING around in outrageous outfits under a sawn-off hairstyle, punk rocker Jason Crompton drove his mother to despair.

But yesterday she was smiling with pride as she watched him, ramrod-stiff and immaculately turned-out, become a Coldstream Guardsman.

'He looks wonderful,' said Mrs Dawn Crompton, from Bolton, after the two-hour passing-out parade at Pirbright, Surrey. 'It's a very special day for me.'

Jason, who is 19 on Monday, used to leap around the stage in a punk group after he was made redundant as an upholsterer.

'He shaved the sides of his head,' added his mother. 'The hair that was left hung over his eyes so he couldn't see his dinner. He used to look so shocking I would tell him to wait until dark before he went out.'

Drifting

All that changed when he met a former fellow-punk, Philip Sharples, in the street. Philip was about to begin a career in the Guards.

'I realised I had been drifting with no real ambition,' said Jason, who dreamed of being a soldier when he was small but then went off the idea. 'I decided it was time to do something with my life and I fancied the challenge of the Army.'

He had no hesitation about which regiment to join. The Coldstream Guards, founded in 1650 by Oliver Cromwell, have claims to be the oldest of the Guards regiments —

By ANNA PUKAS

though the Grenadiers traditionally dispute this.

'When I went to the Army recruitment office last August, I decided to go for the best,' said Jason. 'I didn't want to be half-hearted and I wanted a regiment with a tough reputation. Luckily, I got in. I needed the discipline. After shocking my mum in my punk stage, I'm glad I can make her proud of me.'

On Wednesday Jason will begin an eight-month tour with the First Battalion in Hongkong, where he intends to surprise his friend Philip who has no idea he has joined the Guards.

Then he will return to Wellington Barracks in London and put on the bearskin and red tunic for ceremonial duties including Trooping the Colour.

He has even influenced his 16-year-old sister Joanne, who is thinking of joining the Military Police.

THE GUARD: Jason celebrates with mother after the parade

Picture: DAVID CRUMP

(from the *Daily Mail*, 23 May 1987)

Source B: 'The Summer of Acid House Hype'

Every generation finds its cult. And when Acid House arrived in London in 1988, to the thousands of adolescents who had not been part of one before, it was perfect. It came complete with its own music, its own dress codes, a brand new drug called Ecstacy and, most importantly of all, the promise of a good time.

Its dress code of T-shirt, bandana, baggy shorts or jeans and trainers is an anti-fashion statement – beachwear derived from the come-as-you-are Ibizan discos.

Acid House (the music) and Ecstacy (a class-A prohibited substance) became bound together and the fans turned to it. If they had been born ten years earlier they would have been punk rockers and sniffed glue; if they had been born twenty years earlier they would have taken LSD and listened to the Doors. The song was essentially the same, except this time it was pumped out of disco speakers at about 128 beats per minute.

By July, word had filtered out from the style and music magazines to the national media – in a fallow time for news it was looking for a high too. The quality press documented the phenomenon, News at Ten poked gentle fun at it and the tabloid press just became confused and then hysterical.

In October, the *Sun's* Bizarre column ran a feature about 'groovy and cool' Acid House with a 'guide to the lingo' and a special offer to its readers to buy an Acid House T-shirt for 'only £5.50, man'. Yet just one week later a full-page news story revealed that Ecstacy was a danger drug that was ruining lives.

As a result of this story, Sir Ralph Halpern, boss of Burton Shops, withdrew Smiley motif T-shirts from all 650 stores in his Top Shop chain. Ironically though, largely due to press publicity, Acid House had caught on from Bournemouth to Birkenhead.

(adapted from *The Sunday Times*, 30 October 1988)

Source C

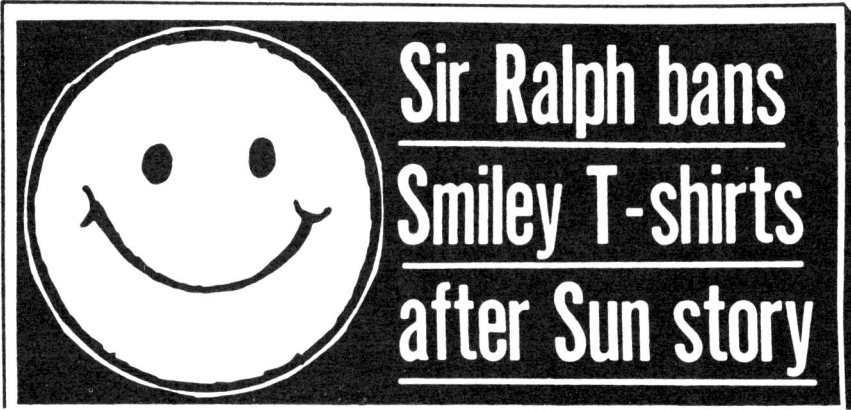

Sir Ralph bans Smiley T-shirts after Sun story

(from the *Sun*, 20 October 1988)

Data-response questions

Using Sources A, B and C:
1 Why did Jason decide to become a soldier?
2 What were the effects of the media's 'moral panic' about Acid House?
3 In what ways was Acid House similar to previous youth cults?
4 What are the limitations of using the above case studies as sociological evidence?

Discussion

'Teenagers today are too concerned about qualifications, careers and financial success to become seriously involved in youth cults.'

Research suggestion

Hypothesis: Teenagers often rebel against the rules and values of their parents but membership of youth subcultures usually only lasts for a year or two.
Method: Ask a sample of adults how far and for how long they rebelled as teenagers.

Youth and old age

People not 'pensioners'

Source A: Marie

Marie looks about seventy but is in fact only fifty. Poverty and hard conditions have caused her to age prematurely.
(from *New Internationalist*, no. 74, April 1979; photo: Camera Press)

Source B: Shirali Muslimov

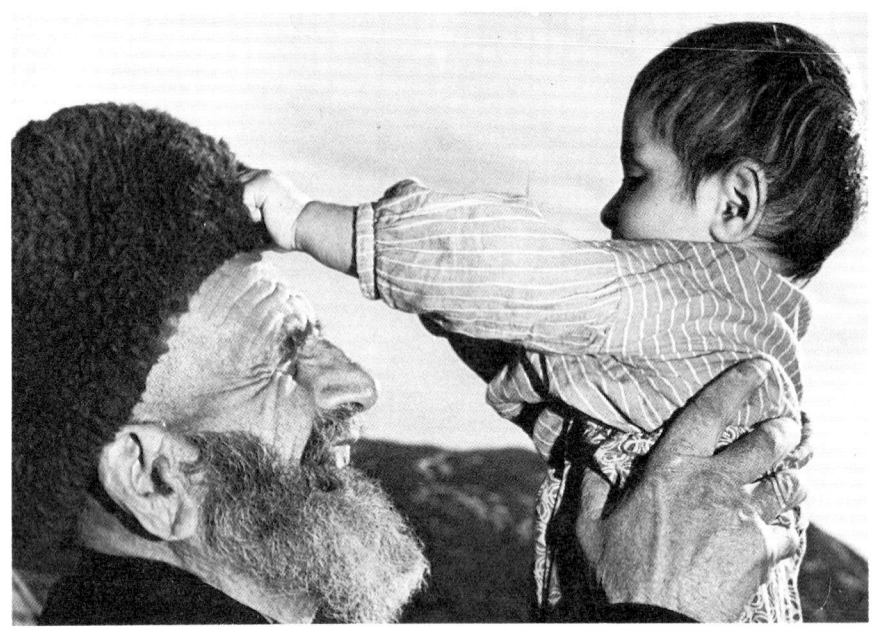

Shirali claims to be 158 years old. In fact he is probably not much over 100, but he looks 50. Pictured here with his youngest descendant, Shirali has been married three times, has had 23 children and now has 150 direct descendants.
(from *New Internationalist*, no. 74, April 1979; photo: Camera Press)

Source C

RETIREMENT
— THE END OF THE ROAD OR A NEW BEGINNING?

(from *People Not 'Pensioners'*, Help the Aged, 1986)

Youth and old age

Source D: A letter to a problem page in a women's magazine

Six months after his retirement, my husband is a changed man. But it's not a change for the better. He has always been active and aware but now it's as if he's stunned. He just sits there staring at the wall. He's always hungry, in fact he's over-eating, as if the food has no taste and he goes on and on about 'not feeling up to anything'. He can't concentrate and is not interested in anything. For him, life has come to an end – which makes a terrifying prospect for me.

(from *People Not 'Pensioners'*)

Source E

(Sources C, D and E are from *People not 'pensioners'* produced by Help the Aged, 1986. The address of Help the Aged's Education Department is 16–18, St James's Walk, London EC1 OBE.)

(from *People Not 'Pensioners'*)

Data-response questions

1 Using Sources A and B, explain the point that 'biological age is not the same thing as chronological age'.
2 If you had to reply to the writer of Source D,
   (a) how would you help her to understand her husband's behaviour?
   (b) what advice would you give?
3 With reference to all the sources, write a short essay discussing the problems which many 'over-sixties' have to face in our society.

Discussion

Some primary schools have invited local over-sixties to help in lessons and ask each to 'adopt' a 'substitute grandchild' from among the pupils. How could this benefit both generations (as well as the teachers!)?

Research suggestion

Hypothesis: People of retirement age are either stereotyped or ignored by advertisers.
Method: Look at advertisements on TV or in magazines (such as colour supplements) which cater for all ages. How many feature over-sixties? Is this the same proportion as the percentage of over-sixties in the general population? What sort of advertisements feature the elderly? How are they portrayed?

4 The family

Changes in family life

Source **A:** The rise in divorce

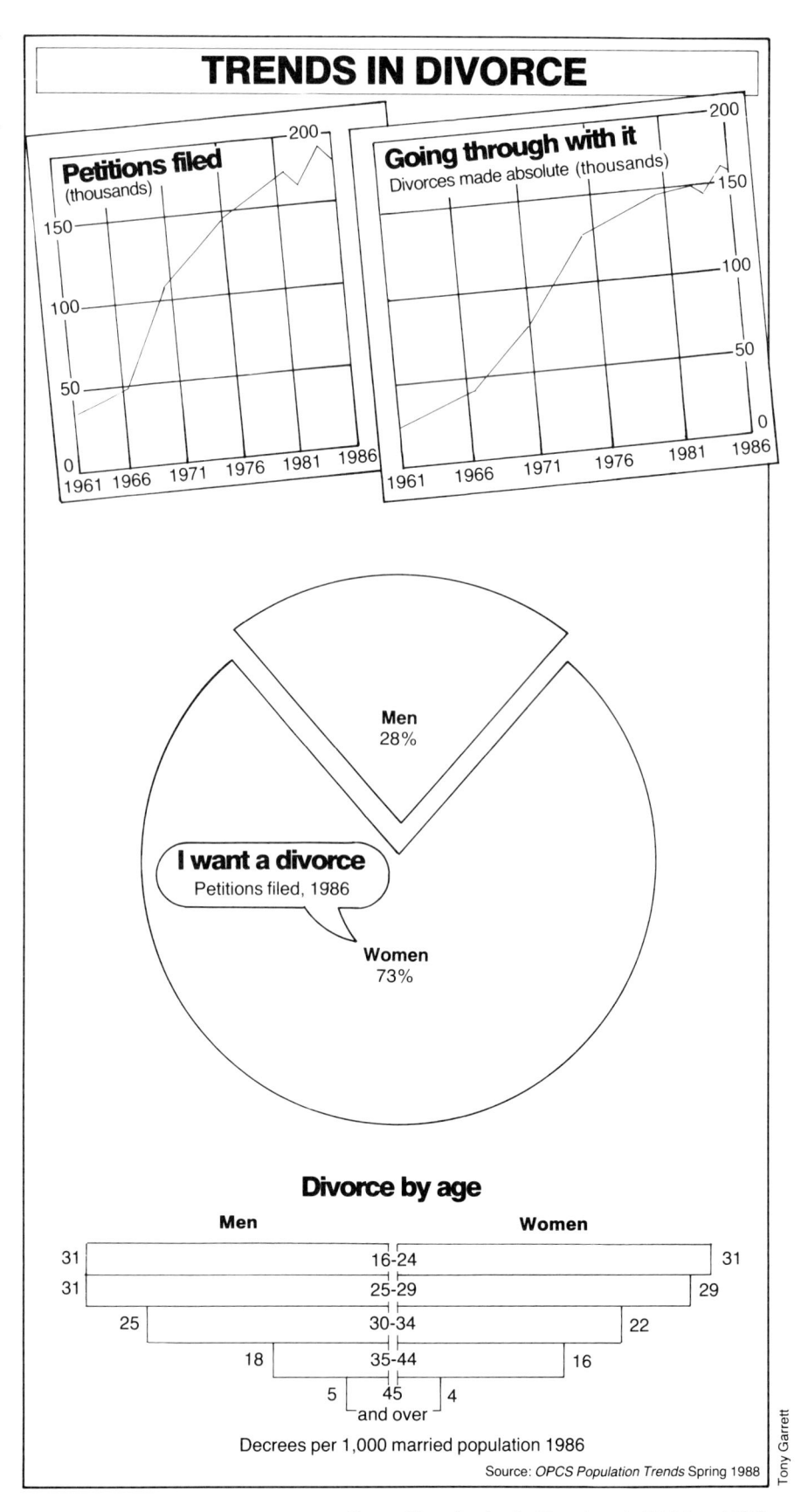

TRENDS IN DIVORCE

Petitions filed (thousands) — 1961 to 1986

Going through with it — Divorces made absolute (thousands), 1961 to 1986

I want a divorce — Petitions filed, 1986
- Men 28%
- Women 73%

Divorce by age

Men	Age	Women
31	16–24	31
31	25–29	29
25	30–34	22
18	35–44	16
5	45 and over	4

Decrees per 1,000 married population 1986

Source: *OPCS Population Trends* Spring 1988

Tony Garrett

(from *New Society's* 'Database', 27 May 1988)

The family

Source B: Illegitimate live births as a percentage of all live births

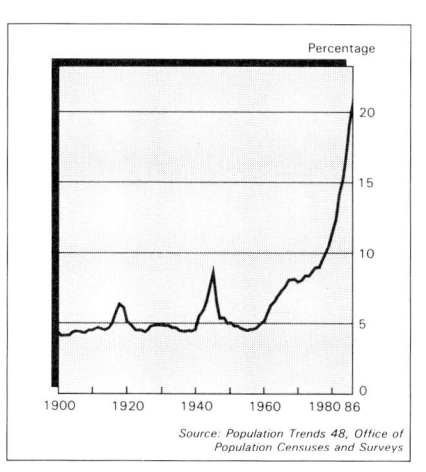

(from Social Trends, 1988)

Source: Population Trends 48, Office of Population Censuses and Surveys

Source C: Households, by size

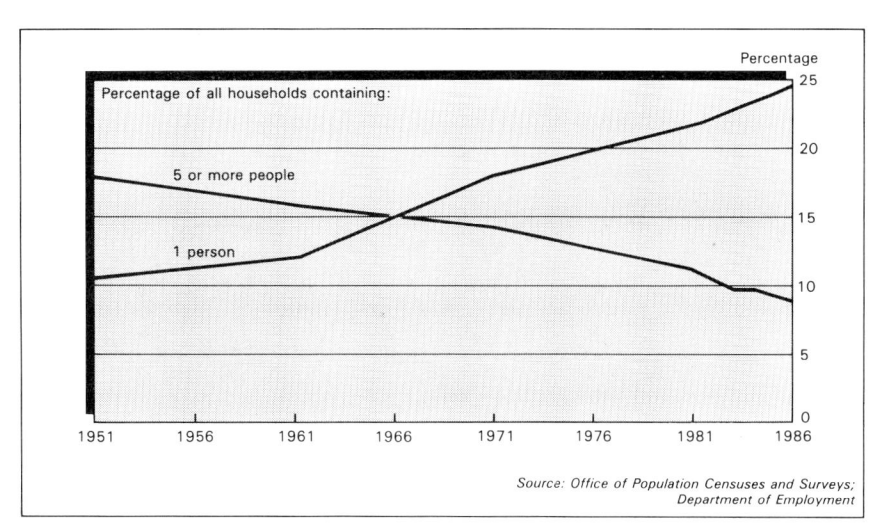

Percentage of all households containing:
- 5 or more people
- 1 person

Source: Office of Population Censuses and Surveys; Department of Employment

(from Social Trends, 1988)

Source D: Students in higher education, by sex

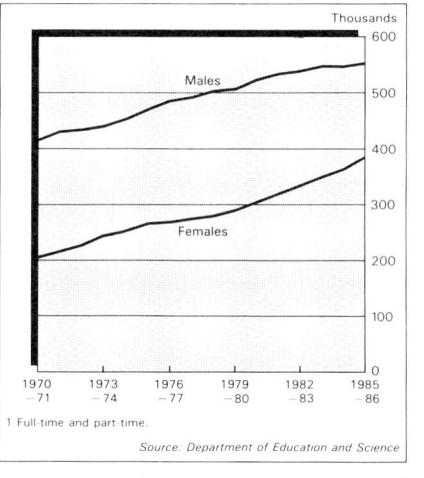

1 Full-time and part-time.
Source: Department of Education and Science

(from Social Trends, 1988)

Source E: Expectation of life at birth, by sex

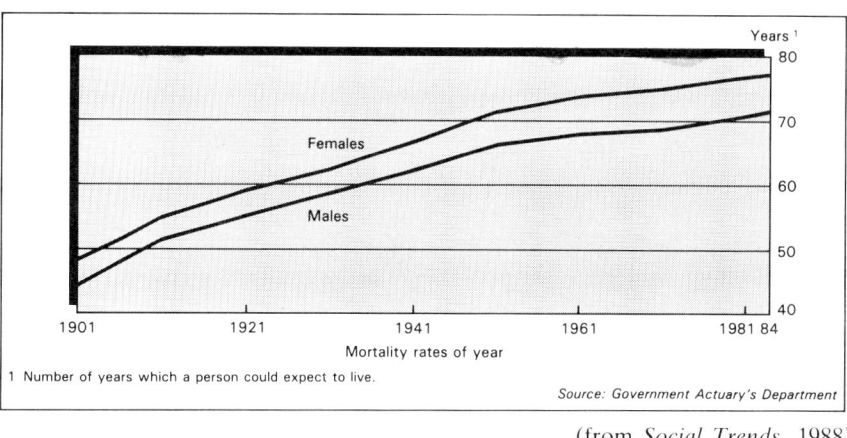

1 Number of years which a person could expect to live.
Source: Government Actuary's Department

(from Social Trends, 1988)

Source F: Saving time, percentage of households

Saving time — Percentage of households

- Microwaves: 2.7% (1982) → 24.7% (1987)
- Dishwashers: 3.1% (1982) → 6.0% (1987)
- Tumble dryers: 19.8% (1982) → 30.5% (1987)

Source: OPCS Population Trends Spring 1988

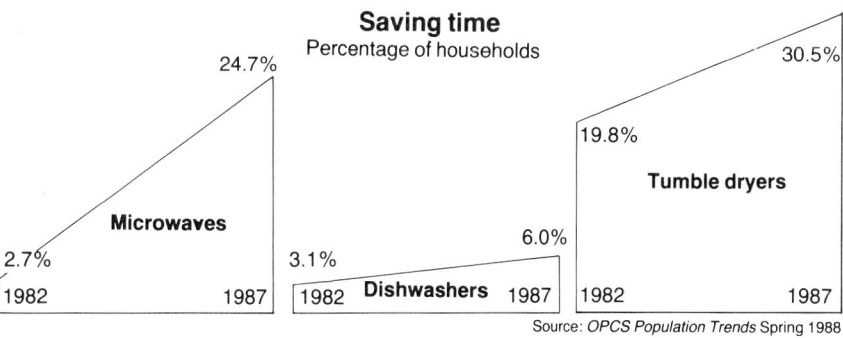

(from New Society's 'Database', 13 May 1988)

Q Data-response question

Write a short essay describing how family life in the United Kingdom has changed as a result of the trends described in Sources A to F.

Types of families

Source A

THOSE LOVELY FOLKS FROM NORMALTOWN

(speech bubbles: "WE MUST BE THE HAPPIEST FAMILY IN BRITAIN!!" / "WE DRIVE A NEW FORD ESCORT AND EARN ENOUGH TO PAY A HEFTY MORTGAGE!" / "WE SHOP AT SAINSBURY, MOTHERCARE AND NEXT!" / BILL £90)

(from *New Society*, 10 April 1987)

Source B: One-parent families

Most one-parent families are poor. The 1984 Family Expenditure Survey shows that on average the total weekly income of a one-parent family was less than half that of a comparable two-parent family. One-parent families are poor because a high proportion of them (51% in 1983) are dependent on Supplementary Benefit and because nearly 90% of them are headed by women, so those that are able to obtain employment are likely to be low-paid. Women still earn only 66% of men's wages. Amongst one-parent families, those headed by unmarried mothers are especially likely to be poor. A very high proportion of single mothers, for example, are dependent on Supplementary Benefit. In 1983, it was 80%. This compares with 42% of divorced mothers and 6.7% of widowed mothers. One of the common problems facing one-parent families is being caught in the double trap of either being poor on social security or impoverished by paying for childcare when working. The following is a letter written by a woman who is head of a single-parent family.

'I had a well-paid job and when I found I was pregnant, a friend said she'd look after the baby. After a very short time she started messing me about, ringing up Sunday evening to say she couldn't look after my daughter the next week. I was in a terrible state. I had to take sick leave to look after my daughter and then get someone else to mind her and this constant change of minder upset the child. She became very fretful. Also, I was paying twice, and when I was already short of money, it meant I only ate dinners two or three times a week. As a result of this and the stress I lost one and a half stone in a month. Last winter when it was cold, I used to take the baby out when it was really cold indoors, so when we got back it would feel warm, as I couldn't afford heating all day and used to have it on one hour in the morning and one hour at night just before the baby went to bed.'

(adapted from *Illegitimate: The Experience of People Born Outside Marriage*, edited by Deborah Derrick, National Council for One Parent Families, 1986)

Source C: The advantages of single-parent families

The presence of two parents does not guarantee better care for the children. In fact, marital breakdown can enable the remaining parent to devote more resources, both material and emotional, to the children. Similarly the presence of a high wage earner does not ensure a high standard of living for all the family. Money can be distributed in such a way that there is 'poverty amidst plenty'. One parent may be well provided for while the spouse and children go short.

One compensation for being a single parent is that there is opportunity to be closer to the children. There is no second adult in the household with whom parenthood must be shared, to whom loyalty is owed, who distracts the parent's attention and discourages the development of separate understandings with the children.

(from *Women, Health and the Family* by Hilary Graham, Wheatsheaf Books, 1984)

Source D: Types of stepfamilies

The proportion of all marriages which are remarriages for one or both parties has increased steadily since the 1969 Divorce Reform Act came into effect in 1971. In 1981 over 33 per cent of all marriages included at least one remarried partner. *Making A Go Of It* (Routledge & Kegan Paul, 1984) is a study of forty stepfamilies in Sheffield. The authors, J. Burgoyne and D. Clark, put the stepfamilies into five categories:

1 'Not really a stepfamily'
With very young children involved, some remarried couples were able to think of themselves as 'just an ordinary family' quite quickly.

2 'Looking forward to the departure of their children'
Some older couples looked forward to their teenage children leaving home so that they could enjoy their new partnership more fully.

3 The 'progressive' stepfamily
Some middle-class informants stressed the importance of change and personal growth in adult life. They did not worry about failing to match the conventional norms of family life. They saw positive values in their decisions to differ from the norm and welcomed the diversity of patterns in modern family and domestic life.

4 The successful pursuit of an 'ordinary' family life
An example is stepfathers who succeed in becoming 'social' fathers to their stepchildren by transferring allegiances from any non-custodial children of an earlier marriage.

5 The conscious pursuit of an 'ordinary' family life frustrated
Financial problems and disputes with the children's non-custodial parent over property, custody and access may frustrate attempts to 'settle down'.

Data-response questions

1 How would you describe the attitude to the 'ordinary family' shown in Source A?
2 Using Source B:
   (a) Give two reasons why many one-parent families are poor.
   (b) Which group of single-parent families is particularly likely to be poor?
3 Using Source C, why might children be better off in single-parent families?
4 Using Source D:
   (a) Why has there been a rise in the number of stepfamilies since 1971?
   (b) What sort of difficulties are mentioned which may be common to stepfamilies?

Discussion

1 'The emotional needs of a child can be as fully met within a single-parent family as within a two-parent family.'
2 'One good aspect of our society is that we are more tolerant of social arrangements and individuals that differ from the recognised, traditional norm than societies in the past.'

Research suggestion

Provide a detailed comparison of the family lives of a one-parent and a two-parent family. A variety of methods could be used including questionnaires, in-depth interviews and perhaps participant observation.

Caring for relatives

Source A: Family ties

Free babysitting, gifts large and small, the loan of the deposit on a first home, caring in times of illness – this kind of help and support appears to be the essence of family life to many people. The expectation that such help will be reliably provided marks the distinguishing line between kinship and other kinds of social relations, including friendship. But are people now less willing than they used to be to deliver this kind of assistance in practice? Do people still feel a special sense 'of obligation' to assist their kin?

The available evidence is that very large numbers of people – mainly women – are providing substantial support for their relatives – especially for elderly parents. Why is it that women in particular continue to provide care? Is it because they feel they 'ought to' or because they 'have to'?

Because women are culturally defined as people who care in our society, the decision about whether to care for an infirm relative – and most particularly a decision *not* to provide care – is very different for a woman and a man in equivalent positions. Quite simply, men have many more available reasons which others will accept as legitimate for not providing such support.

People's decisions and actions about assisting their relatives may stem partly from beliefs, but those beliefs have to be applied in particular circumstances, and socio-economic conditions have changed in important ways. To take just two examples:

1. On the one hand, we have many more people surviving into old age where they need substantial care; those elderly people have fewer children who might be able to share parental care; and hardly any of them have never-married daughters who at certain times in the past were prime targets for cooption as carers.
2. On the other hand, changed patterns of public provision have meant that there is a different range of alternatives to family care available, at least in principle. This makes a decision about offering care for a relative different from in the past, when the only possible alternative – the workhouse – was regarded by most people as unthinkable, and indeed was designed to be so.

(adapted from 'Family Ties' by Janet Finch, in *New Society*, 20 March 1987)

It has been estimated that at least three-quarters of the people who act as 'main carers' are women; while men may care for a disabled or infirm wife, they are unlikely to do so for other relatives.

Mrs Pat Ward and her mother are helped by a carers scheme which gives Mrs Ward a few hours off each week.

Source B: The reality of community care

The great majority of those in need of care, be they the elderly, the physically or mentally handicapped or the mentally ill, receive it within the context of their family. This pattern has been encouraged by the increased emphasis given recently to community, as distinct from institutional, care. The first community care policies, in the late 1950s, stressed small-scale homes run by paid staff and located within the community (as opposed to large, geographically isolated institutions). In the 1980s the focus has been on care *by* rather than just *in* the community. The theory is that those in need can be kept out of residential homes by a network of informal carers – kin, friends, neighbours, volunteers – backed up by local social and medical services.

In practice, community care usually boils down to little more than family care, with relatively little help being given by those outside the household. Indeed within households there is a marked division of labour in tending, as in other domestic matters, with the primary carer normally being a close female relative: mothers, wives and daughters. Men are usually involved to a much lesser degree, except in cases where husbands are looking after their handicapped wives.

One study of the care given to elderly relatives found that wives spent some two to three hours per day in caring tasks compared to their husbands' eight minutes. Broadly similar findings are reported in studies of the care given to handicapped children.

The burden of caring for an elderly relative can undoubtedly become a very heavy one. The primary carer – normally a wife, daughter or daughter-in-law – is herself likely to be of retirement age when the elderly person in question needs the most support. The tiredness and strain of being constantly on call, of having to lift the elderly person regularly, of having sleep continually broken, etc., not only limits opportunities for leisure and social involvement, but can also result in high degrees of friction within the household. Gradually as the tending required becomes more extensive, it comes to dominate the carer's identity.

Carers need to be able to recuperate from the burden of their work and they also need to be able to maintain a life of their own. Imaginative schemes of domiciliary and out-care services are required (not just meals-on-wheels, luncheon clubs and home-helps, but night nurses, day hospitals and respite care). Such schemes of course require extensive funding and are thus unlikely to be developed very fully under present economic policies. With current provision, informal family care is cheap for the government but the cost can be very heavy for those doing the caring.

(adapted from 'The Family' by G. Allen, *Inside British Society* edited by G. A. Causer, 1987)

Data-response questions

1 Using Source A, why was it more common in the past for daughters to care for those parents who survived into old age?
2 Using Source B:
   (a) List some of the types of institutions which have been widely used for 'institutional care' in the past.
   (b) How have ideas of 'community care' changed from the 1950s to the 1980s?
   (c) What have been the findings of studies into the division of labour between husband and wife carers?
   (d) What can be done to help those who offer domiciliary care (care in their own homes) to needy relatives?
3 Why have the numbers of old people in Britain increased?
4 Why does the burden of caring for elderly parents fall more heavily on daughters than on sons?

Discussion

How well do we care for our own elderly relatives and neighbours?

Research suggestion

Hypothesis: Assistance for elderly parents is widespread among families and this assistance takes many forms (which vary according to class and ethnicity).
Method: Interview a sample of families about their contact with and care for elderly parents.

Divorce

Source A: Divorce has been a popular method of ending marriages in most societies for much of human history

An idea common in almost all pre-Christian and non-Christian societies is that any serious conception of marriage must include provision for ending disastrous marriages. Furthermore, the regular and universal feature of such societies is the relative ease of divorce. Certainly in Western Europe, what marks out the Christian era from earlier and later times is the insistence that marriage should be 'till death us do part'. It is this which makes the dramatic contrast with the marriage customs of virtually all the peoples who were to be Christianised over the centuries; the Romans no less than the Anglo-Saxons, the Celts no less than most of the inhabitants of Africa and Asia who were to be converted by missionaries a thousand years later. Only the Hindus seem to have maintained anything like the strictness of the Catholic Church towards divorce.

These marriage customs were so different that it was often centuries before the Christians managed to exert effective control. Take the example of Ireland: in our time, Ireland has been the most uniformly obedient daughter of the Church and even today has not followed the rest of Northern Europe in relaxing the law of divorce. Yet in ancient Ireland, centuries after the conversion to Christianity, divorce was freely allowed. A marriage might always be ended by mutual consent. Similarly, in mediaeval Wales, the couple might, in practice, separate at the will of either or by mutual consent; the division of the household goods depended on the time and circumstances of the separation, the length of the marriage, the cause of the split and so on. Custody of the children was divided between the parents.

Pre-Christian societies in general recognise two rights: the underlying right of individuals to divorce and remarry, and the right to compensation and maintenance of those adversely affected by the divorce. The right of divorce was gradually eroded by the Church in its long struggle to gain control of matrimony.

(adapted from *The Subversive Family* by Ferdinand Mount, Counterpoint, 1982)

Source B: The joys of family life are largely reserved for the better off

The quality of relationships between husbands and wives is rarely seen as having anything to do with economic, material conditions. Thus politicians like to believe that the deepening social divisions within our society have little effect on the essentials of family life. It is those who have close, daily contact with families other than their own who know otherwise. Health visitors, doctors and social workers are easily made aware that the emotional and the material are in fact two sides of the same coin. To these groups the fact that divorce rates are four times higher in social class V than among professional groups, and highest of all among the unemployed will come as no surprise. Happy relationships between husbands and wives are dependent to an important extent on the achievement of socially acceptable standards of living. Since 1945 what we consider an acceptable standard of living has gone up and up. And with it has similarly increased the likelihood of divorce among couples who fail to achieve what we consider an acceptable way of life.

Housing provides a good case in point. The ideal of 'having a place of one's own' has become increasingly popular, an increasingly valued investment in both an emotional and a material sense. In sometimes unconscious and very subtle ways home ownership creates a sense of security as well as offering tax advantages for those with assured incomes. Those who still do not own their homes may now feel that they are depriving themselves and their children of one of the basic building blocks of family life.

The poorer members of society compete at the very bottom of the housing market where they are frequently forced into buying housing in need of repair on a maximum mortgage. They are also more likely to be amongst the groups at greatest risk of falling behind with their repayments as a result of unemployment or some other financial setback. The 1987 edition of *Social Trends* includes data from the Building Societies Association which shows a very substantial and alarming increase in the number of property repossessions in the period of the Thatcher government. In 1979 there were 2,500 repossessions; by 1985 this figure had reached almost 17,000. How many stories of marital stress and marital breakdown does this figure contain?

(adapted from 'Material Happiness' by Jacqueline Burgoyne, *New Society*, 10 April 1987)

The family

Source C: Divorce statistics by duration of marriage

Great Britain
Percentages and numbers

Year of divorce	0–2	3–4	5–9	10–14	15–19	20–24	25–29	30 +	All divorces (= 100%) (numbers)
1961	1.2	10.1	30.6	22.9	13.9	21.2			27,018
1971	1.2	12.2	30.5	19.4	12.6	9.5	5.8	8.9	79,249
1976	1.5	16.5	30.2	18.7	12.8	8.8	5.6	5.9	135,386
1979	1.2	17.4	30.4	19.0	12.4	8.9	5.2	5.6	147,539
1980	1.3	17.8	30.4	19.3	12.5	8.6	5.0	5.0	158,831
1981	1.5	18.0	30.1	19.4	12.7	8.6	5.0	4.7	155,608
1982	1.5	19.0	29.1	19.6	12.8	8.6	4.9	4.5	157,986
1983	1.3	19.5	28.7	19.2	12.9	8.6	5.2	4.7	160,717
1984	1.2	19.6	28.3	18.9	13.2	8.7	5.3	4.6	156,416
1985	8.9	18.8	26.2	17.1	12.3	7.9	4.7	4.2	173,673

Duration of marriage (completed years)

(from *Social Trends*, 1987)

Data-response questions

1 Using Source A:
   (a) What is the universal feature of pre-Christian and non-Christian societies?
   (b) Explain in your own words the meaning of the opening sentence.
   (c) How did couples in mediaeval Wales obtain a divorce?
   (d) In what ways is historical knowledge, of the type presented in this source, helpful to us?
   (e) What attitude to the Church is expressed by the writer?

2 Using Source B:
   (a) What, besides emotional factors, has an important effect on marital relationshps?
   (b) Which social class has the highest divorce rate?
   (c) What explanation does the writer put forward to account for this?

3 Using Source C:
   (a) How many more divorces were there in 1985 compared to 1961?
   (b) In 1982 what percentage of divorces were between couples whose marriages had lasted five to nine years?
   (c) Give three reasons, explaining each fully, to account for the increase in divorce.

Discussion

1 'The quality of married life has been improved by the availability of divorce.'

2 'Divorce is the ending of a very private relationship between two individuals and therefore neither governments nor churches should try to make it harder to obtain.'

Research suggestion

Hypothesis: People expect more from marriage now than those who got married thirty or forty years ago.

Method: Prepare a questionnaire for a sample of young and a sample of old people. Arrange in-depth interviews with a number of young married couples and with couples who have been married for thirty years or more.

Gender roles in Britain and the USSR

Source **A**: All work and no play

All work and no play — that's the life for today's stay-at-home housewives

by MARGARET HENFIELD

A WOMAN'S place is still in the home — especially at night, according to a survey.

Mothers may be allowed to bring in extra money to help feed and clothe the children, but requests for a night out meet stony silence, sulking and a refusal to babysit from husbands.

And the depressing truth for feminists is that most housewives accept their lot. Running a home and caring for a family is so hectic they hardly have time to take a break.

They expect their husbands to enjoy a drink in the pub with the boys, but don't count on equal leisure time for themselves, it is claimed.

The survey of 700 women and their partners was carried out by Eileen Green, Sandra Hebron and Diana Woodward, of Sheffield Polytechnic, with the help of research secretary Viv Mallinder.

Almost half the women questioned said they had too little time to take part in sport or social activities away from the home. But their men made time for squash, football, hobbies and drinking sessions.

Miss Green, a senior lecturer in sociology, explained: 'With some women, leisure time simply meant having five minutes for a cup of tea away from the children.

'Some men were worried about their partners going out without them for a drink because they might meet other men — so jealousy creeps in.'

But most of the women interviewed were not angry about their stay-at-home existence. 'It was commonplace to them,' said Miss Green. 'It's what they expected in many senses. We were quite depressed by the end of it.'

Working class women and those with unemployed partners fared worst in the leisure stakes.

While many middle-class housewives owned or could use a car, women from lower income families had to take public transport to make a fleeting escape from house and family.

'Those with unemployed partners were under the most stress,' said Miss Green.

'Though you would expect them to have had more time to help with the children and housework, the men did not want to be seen to be doing womens' work. In fact many got in the way of the women's leisure time in the home.'

As well as their partners' jealousy, cash was a problem too. Husbands set aside part of their income for leisure but wives felt guilty about using house-keeping money for fun.

Miss Green said: 'They felt they were not entitled to the money — so they ended up needing support, permission and economic resources from their partners to enable them to go out.'

(from the *Daily Mail*, 14 May 1987)

Source **B**: Many families cling to traditional gender roles, even when the man is out of work

The most dramatic change to have occurred in British society over the last two decades is the almost continual rise in male unemployment. Alongside male job loss, however, we have seen a steady growth in the numbers of married women in the workforce. These trends raise a number of obvious questions about the way in which recent economic change is affecting the nuclear family household, traditionally assumed to be maintained by the family wage of a sole male breadwinner. A popular conclusion has been that men and women are 'swapping roles'. Much more significant than role reversal, however, is the polarisation of society into two-earner homes and no-earner homes.

The two-earner household pattern that is emerging does not seem to effect a major change in perceptions of women's role within the home. The fact that women's income, especially from part-time work, is unlikely to rival that of their husband's means that there is no significant challenge to the notion of the male breadwinner. Women's earnings are popularly seen as providing 'pin-money'. And yet it has been shown that without such an income the number of households in poverty would increase threefold.

But what is the situation in homes where the man is out of work? Research into this question has repeatedly discovered that male unemployment is likely to carry with it a resistance on the part of the man to any suggestion that he should take over domestic chores. His identity, already threatened by job loss, will be further threatened by 'women's work'.

Unemployment is overwhelmingly concentrated amongst the unskilled and semi-skilled within the working class. It is also the case that predominantly working-class areas are characterised by particular ideas about the nature of appropriate male and female behaviour. My interviews in the households of redundant steelworkers in South Wales have demonstrated this: 'He doesn't like housework anyway. I suppose he thinks it is not manly. He'd dust and tidy downstairs but he won't do upstairs because no one sees it, and he won't clean the windows in case the neighbours see him.' Many women felt that to organise a reluctant husband into performing domestic tasks was more costly in terms of strain on herself and the marriage than to perform the tasks herself.

(adapted from 'The No-Longer Working Class' by Lydia Morris in *New Society*, April 1987)

Source C: Gender roles in the USSR

Soviet women have long had the right to work in production, on a par with men. Women constitute 51 per cent of personnel in the national economy and 53 per cent of the population. Also, 60 per cent of women have a specialised secondary or higher education. This means that women not only have the right to work but use this right extensively. The Soviet Union has long acheived the aim of many countries – to provide jobs for all women who wish to work. But our rapid advance in this sphere has put up many problems before society. The most acute are:

- Many women have to carry a double burden – at work and in the family;
- Many women work at enterprises with tiring working conditions, or do monotonous, dull or low paid work;
- Many men do not help in the family with children or household chores. This is not only because they are 'male chauvinists' but also because they have to work very hard to provide for the family – unfortunately, living standards in the Soviet Union are not very high;
- It is still a problem to get a large flat, an essential condition for a normal family life. And the chances of getting or buying a larger flat are better if both husband and wife work.

The result had been the dwindling birth rate that was checked last year. Had the birth rate continued to dwindle, the question whould have been not who should opt for childcare but whom to bring up. Where is the way out? We should create conditions for women to have a free choice. Families themselves should choose who would opt for childcare – man or woman. But society should create conditions where work would not be an economic necessity for women. Several measures are suggested for achieving this goal and the most important are:

- To greatly raise wages for men so that their wives can choose whether to work or not to work;
- To create conditions for mothers to be able to work a shorter week or flexitime, and to take leave for an indefinite period for childcare;
- To increase annual paid leave both for men and women;
- To pay mothers the salary they drew at their latest place of work until their child is eight or ten years old, and their service record should not be broken;
- To give newlyweds, irrespective of their service record, age or material status, a flat that would allow them to have two or three children;
- To bring up children (especially boys) in a way that, when they grow up to have families, either of the spouses would use the right to opt for childcare.

These and other suggestions involve changing social stereotypes and spending much more money on families.

(adapted from 'Vitali Tretyakov Defends Himself' by Vitali Tretyakov in *Soviet Weekly*, 6 February 1988)

Data-response questions

1 Using Source A, give two reasons why mothers do not have the same amount of leisure time as their husbands.
2 Using Source B:
   (a) How are women's earnings popularly described?
   (b) Explain why this description is in many cases misleading and inaccurate.
   (c) Why are many unemployed husbands unwilling to do housework?
3 Using Source C:
   (a) What is the double burden that women carry?
   (b) Why is it often necessary for both married partners to work in the Soviet Union?
   (c) What problems do women in the Soviet Union and women in this country have in common?

Discussion

Do the experiences of your fellow students support the description of burdened mothers that emerges from these extracts?

Research suggestion

Hypothesis: The symmetrical family with evenly shared conjugal roles is more a myth than a reality.
Method: Prepare a questionnaire for pupils about roles in the home. Arrange in-depth interviews with husbands and wives focusing on domestic chores, childcare, decision-making and attitudes to paid employment.

5 Rural and urban communities

Rural Life

Source **A**

... buying up property that should be occupied by land workers!'

Source **B**: The effects of newcomers on the village community

'Village community' can mean three things:

1 It can mean a type of geographical settlement – a small number of people living together in a rural location.
2 It can mean that everyone knows everyone else – even if they are all at each other's throats – so that the village has a close-knit social pattern.
3 Finally, it can mean that there is a spirit of community, a sense of belonging, of sharing a social identity in a spirit of friendliness and common experience.

Many villages have undergone a changing social composition, but have they lost their community spirit? Such a question assumes that the traditional agricultural village had a community spirit. But such an assumption might merely rest on a glorification of the past. The village inhabitants formed a community in the past because they had to: they were imprisoned by constraints of various kinds, including poverty. Thus helping one another may well have been a necessity. Gossip, bickering and family feuds may well have been more widespread than a happy community spirit.

In the last century many villages were isolated and largely self-contained communities in which most workers were employed either on farms or in crafts associated with agriculture. Members of such villages were often fiercely loyal to their communities. Villages had a clear identity with a clearly defined social and geographical place in society.

Such villages had two layers:

1 the 'official' village community which included landowners, farmers and clergy;
2 the locally-based working-class subculture which excluded 'them' in authority – a neighbourly association of kin and workmates which also excluded outsiders.

Locals and newcomers

Mechanisation has meant fewer jobs available on farms and thus many villagers have left to find work elsewhere. At the same time many villages have, since the 1950s, filled up with urban, middle-class newcomers. These have been either commuters, those in retirement or second-home owners ('weekenders'). The new 'immigrants' do not make the village the focus of all their social activities. As a result, everybody does not know everybody else. The newcomers may have little interest in observing the niceties of village life. The rump of the old occupational community may become a village within a village, suspicious of and resistant to social contact with the outsiders who have invaded 'their' village. Resentment may easily focus on the issue of housing. Cottages which used to be rented cheaply may now be sold for vast sums, while newcomers may oppose the building of new council houses.

(adapted from *Green and Pleasant Land? Social Change in Rural England* by H. Newby, Wildwood House, 1979)

Source C: Boredom in the village

Talking in Tamworth on 5 February, the Home Secretary reminded us that hooliganism and vandalism were not inner city specialities: 'Recent disturbances in shire areas have been largely caused by youths who are white, employed, well-off and drunk.'

I live in Suffolk and I am one of the few able-bodied adults to use the bus service that runs from Ipswich to Sudbury, via Hadleigh. In both the last named towns, the bus stations have in the last ten years been reconstructed more than once, with the soundest architectural advice, when their vandalisation became too sordid to be ignored. The unbreakable non-glass replacements at Hadleigh were long ago destroyed and the shelter rebuilt, but the first round of the new vandal-proof seating there has already been triumphantly removed. Visiting equally well-off Hampshire, I found that everyone had the same story. If you ask young people why their peers break up the bus shelter, they reply with the word that has been heard for generations: 'boredom'.

In his National Youth Bureau study of Dorset, Allan Kennedy found that most of the needs of children up to the age of fourteen were being met, and that 'in the summer young people, regardless of their age, are less likely to be at a loss for something to do, but in the winter the situation is sometimes desperate for many older adolescents. For many in Dorset adolescence is a time of isolation and depression'.

It is the same in the little towns and villages round our way. There are fewer buses than at any time in the last sixty years. They are expensive and the last one runs before the evening begins. There are restaurants and wine bars, but nothing cheap. The young who cannot afford the pub hang around pathetically outside the Chinese takeaway, and the only place out of the rain is the bus shelter. Kennedy is right to comment that 'the feeling of depression and the sense of isolation can be seen quite clearly on the faces of many youngsters: lonely people living in one of the most beautiful parts of the country'.

'They'll grow out of it', the parents say, and of course they will. But it isn't much fun to be lacking funds, lacking resources and living in what is for me a rural paradise, but is for them a social desert.

(adapted from 'Village Idiocy' by Colin Ward in *New Society*, 4 March 1988)

Data-response questions

1 What point of view is expressed in Source A?
2 Using Source B:
   (a) Explain the meaning of the phrase 'glorification of the past'.
   (b) What groups within the middle class have recently moved to villages?
   (c) In what way does the way of life of the newcomers differ from that of traditional villagers?
   (d) Why might housing become the focus of conflict between traditional villagers and the newcomers?
3 Using Source C:
   (a) Why are many young people living in small towns and villages bored?
   (b) What do you think could be done to help this group of youngsters to overcome their boredom?

Discussion

'City life is best suited to the young and country life is best suited to the old.'

Research suggestion

Hypothesis: Most young city-dwellers are content to live in the city whilst most middle-aged and old city inhabitants would prefer to live in the country.
Method: Give a questionnaire to a sample of each age-group. Conduct in-depth interviews with a few members from each sample.

Rural and urban communities

Housing patterns

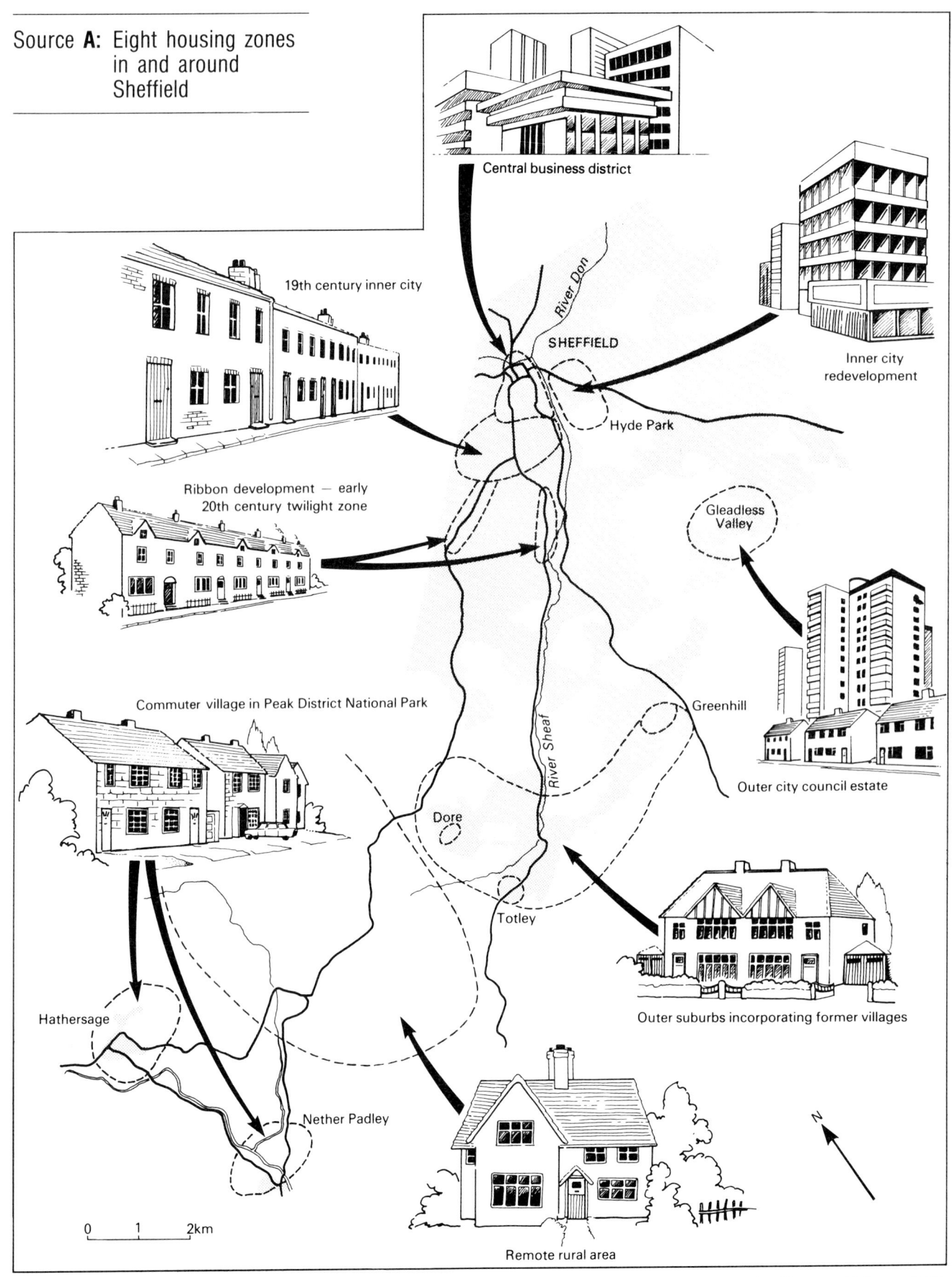

Source **A**: Eight housing zones in and around Sheffield

Central business district

19th century inner city

Inner city redevelopment

SHEFFIELD

Hyde Park

Ribbon development — early 20th century twilight zone

Gleadless Valley

Commuter village in Peak District National Park

Greenhill

Outer city council estate

Dore

Totley

Outer suburbs incorporating former villages

Hathersage

Nether Padley

Remote rural area

0 1 2km

N

(from *The British Isles* by D. Waugh, Thomas Nelson, 1986)

Rural and urban communities

Source B: Housing and class (1984 figures)

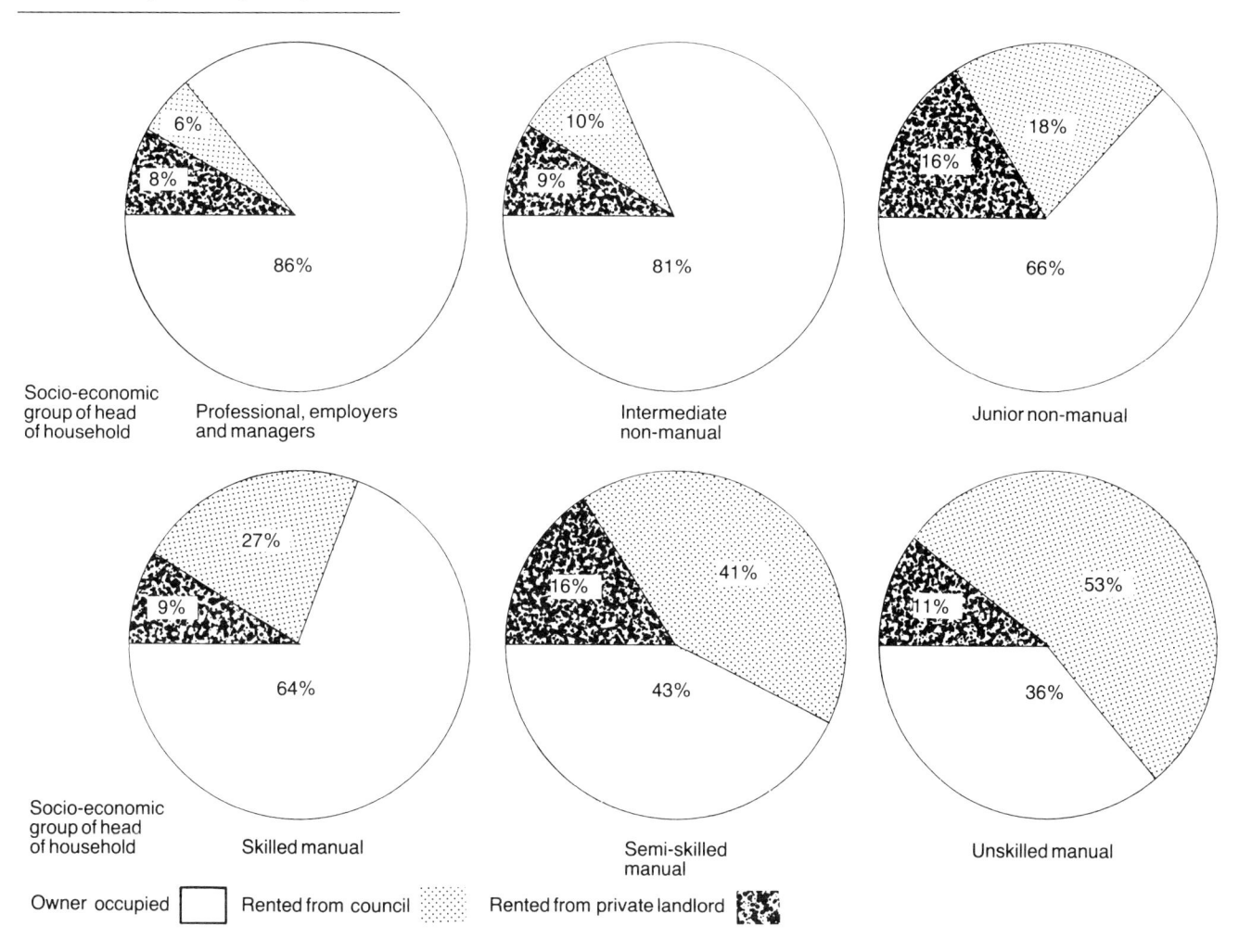

Socio-economic group of head of household:

- **Professional, employers and managers**: 86% owner occupied, 8% rented from private landlord, 6% rented from council
- **Intermediate non-manual**: 81% owner occupied, 9% rented from private landlord, 10% rented from council
- **Junior non-manual**: 66% owner occupied, 16% rented from private landlord, 18% rented from council
- **Skilled manual**: 64% owner occupied, 9% rented from private landlord, 27% rented from council
- **Semi-skilled manual**: 43% owner occupied, 16% rented from private landlord, 41% rented from council
- **Unskilled manual**: 36% owner occupied, 11% rented from private landlord, 53% rented from council

Key: Owner occupied / Rented from council / Rented from private landlord

(adapted from *Social Trends*, 1987)

Data-response questions

1 Using Source A:
  (a) What type of housing is to be found in the Peak District National Park?
  (b) In general, what socio-economic group (class) would you expect to find living in each of the housing districts?
  (c) List the arguments for and against the building of private houses for commuters in National Parks such as in Hathersage.
  (d) What are the arguments for and against building council estates on the edge of big cities?

2 Using Source B:
  (a) What percentage of unskilled manual workers are owner-occupiers?
  (b) Which class has the smallest percentage of council house occupants?

Discussion

'Houses should not be built in Green Belt areas.'

Research suggestion

Carry out research designed to show how and why housing and environmental conditions have changed in your area over the last thirty years. The Planning Office of your local council may be able to offer help on this.

High-rise flats

Source **A**: Inner-city redevelopments

When in the 1950s and 1960s vast areas of inner cities were cleared by bulldozers many of the displaced inhabitants either moved to council estates near the city boundary, or were rehoused in huge high-rise tower blocks which were created on the sites of the old terraced houses (Figure 8.18).

The Cebus Bory Tower block estate was opened in 1968 in the London Borough of Hackney. From the start they were damp and by 1971 many of the seven blocks were uninhabitable. They were dynamited in 1983 and replaced by 'old fashioned' houses with gardens. Other tower blocks, especially on Merseyside have suffered similar fates.

▽ Figure 8.18 High rise flats — Glasgow

The reasons for building high-rise flats were:

- The local authorities found these high-rise flats cheap to build and quick to erect (as were the nineteenth century houses they had replaced).
- To save space by building upwards.
- To create areas of open space between the tower blocks.
- To provide modern indoor amenities such as WCs, hot running water and central heating.
- To provide freedom from industrial traffic and yet to allow easy access to jobs and shops in the nearby CBD.
- To keep together the community spirit of the nineteenth century communities.
- To create panoramic views. (How many storeys do the flats in Figure 8.18 have?)

These high-rise flats were built in good faith for **economic advantage**.

High-rise flats proved to be a failure because:

- Inhuman conditions gave a total lack of neighbourliness.
- These ugly buildings were also surrounded by non-usable areas of open space.
- The elderly felt trapped, especially those living above the ground floors.
- There was a lack of play areas and amenities for youngsters.
- Mugging in passageways prevented many elderly inhabitants venturing out; and there was a high level of vandalism and noise.
- The mental strain and depression amongst the inhabitants rapidly increased.
- The poor quality of the buildings. Indeed, one tower block in London (Ronan Point) collapsed, and several others (e.g. Oak and Eldon flats in Liverpool) were to be demolished.
- There still existed an extremely high population density (e.g. Hyde Park, Sheffield had 400 persons per hectare).

It was only later therefore that the inhabitants found living in the flats to be a social disadvantage.

(from *The British Isles*)

Rural and urban communities

Tower blocks undergoing demolition on the Cantril Farm estate in Liverpool, in 1988.

(from the *Guardian*, 27 April 1988)

Source B: Problems of high-rise flats

There has been growing interest in the social effects of the apparently unowned and unpoliced public walkways, decks, corridors and minimally landscaped recreational areas of large-scale flatted developments. In Britain, Alice Coleman has looked at several indicators of depression and squalor – litter, graffiti, vandal damage, the number of children in care, the presence of urine in public – and related them to the design of the estates. It would be hard to deny that arrogant planning policies and ill-thought-out design have played a big part in creating problems which are now generally recognised.

According to the 1978 General Household Survey, 50 per cent of those interviewed put bungalows at the top of the list of preferred housing type. And although many more would rather be buying than renting (72 per cent compared with 19 per cent) it seemed that the desire to live in a house of reasonable quality was stronger than the desire to buy a house.

(adapted from 'Housing' by A. M. Rees in *Inside British Society* edited by Gordon A. Causer, Wheatsheaf Books, 1987)

Data-response questions

1 Using Source A:
   (a) When were high-rise flats built?
   (b) What was the economic reason for building high-rise flats?
   (c) What problems did old people experience living in this type of dwelling?
   (d) What problems for residents living in high-rise flats are indicated by the photograph?
2 Using Source B, explain the meaning of the phrases 'minimally landscaped recreational areas' and 'arrogant planning policies'.
3 Using both sources, suggest ways to improve the quality of life for residents of 1960s high-rise developments.

Discussion

What can sociologists contribute to the successful redevelopment of run-down inner-city areas?

Research suggestion

Conduct a survey to investigate how far the physical features of a housing estate create problems for the residents.

6 Racism

Types of racism

Source **A**: Racism in South Africa

Welcome greets a white 'outcast'

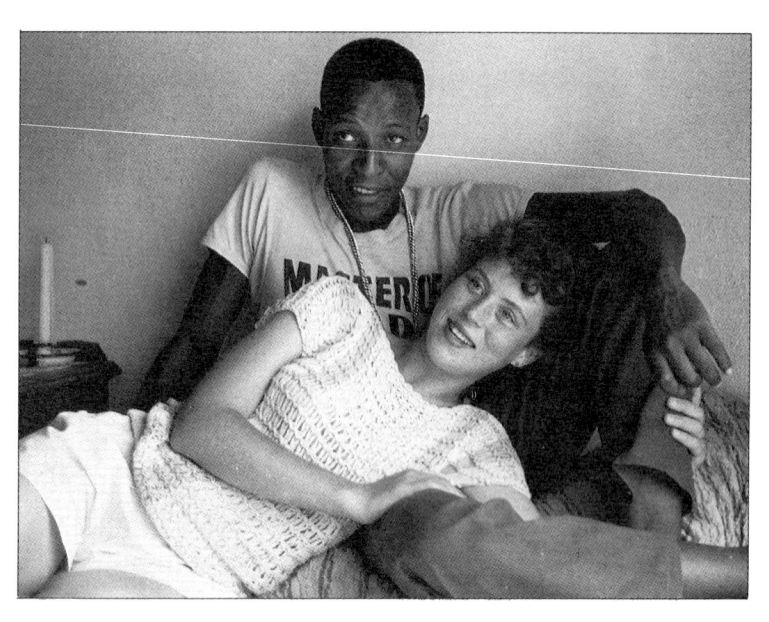

Home is a friendly township: Annette Heunis and Jerry Tsie whom she now plans to marry despite the anger of her family

**by Peter Godwin
Odendaalsrus
Orange Free State**

THOUSANDS of people in a black South African township have "adopted" a young white woman who has chosen to live and marry among them.

Annette Heunis, 20, is shunned by the white community in the segregated country town of Odendaalsrus because she has done the unthinkable by falling in love with a young black man. But she is a heroine to the nearby township folk, and they have nicknamed her Palesa, which means "beloved one" in the local Sotho language.

Although the law banning mixed marriages was struck off the South African statute book two years ago, racial segregation is so ingrained in the remote farmlands of the Orange Free State that Heunis's decision has brought threats and abuse down on her.

She used to be an ordinary Afrikaans girl like hundreds of others in this small conservative town. Her father, "Tiny" Heunis, a great hulk of a man who worked as barman at the whites-only bar of the Outspan Hotel, and her stepmother, Petro, used to keep a very tight rein on their only child and she had no boyfriends.

Then Jerry Tsie, a security guard at a gold mine, walked into the photographic studios where Annette Heunis worked. She lived in a whites-only suburb, had been to a whites-only school and voted in a whites-only election. He was born in a black "compound" which exists outside every South African town, no matter how small. He went to a black township school and had never before socialised with a white person.

From the moment they met she had "a strong feeling for him". Last year he gave her a valentine declaring his love and the two began courting secretly.

When Heunis eloped and swapped her comfortable flat for a crowded tin-roofed house with no electricity in the township of Kutluanong, white Odendaalsrus was appalled.

Tiny Heunis told the police his daughter must have been abducted. Two white constables visited her but she told them she was with Tsie voluntarily.

The couple received more than 10 abusive phone calls a day from irate whites, and Tsie was shot at one day near the town centre. Heunis's stepmother has declared her dead, her furious father called her a whore and her white friends all rejected her. Her old headmaster said she would not be invited to school reunions.

In the township it was different. Thousands of people congregated at the Tsie family house just to catch a glimpse of their first white resident.

The couple plan to marry in the African Methodist church when Heunis turns 21 in November. She has left her old Dutch Reformed Church because, she says, "they would never be happy with this". But she would dearly like a reconciliation with her father.

In the meantime, she dare not go shopping in her home town and both she and Tsie are clearly afraid of attacks by whites.

"Petty apartheid" is alive and well in white Odendaalsrus. When I asked the town secretary what the population was he told me 10,500 people. Then he added that there were also more than 30,000 blacks.

Tsie believes their love has broken new ground: "Whites say it's impossible for blacks to live with whites. We have proved them wrong." Heunis says simply: "I'm here because I love my young man."

(from *The Sunday Times*, 17 January 1988)

Source B: Racial attacks in Britain

An indictment of the policing of racist attacks is contained in 'Racial attacks in Britain: a survey in eight areas in Britain' published by the Commission for Racial Equality in July 1987.

This report highlights the vulnerability of the Black community: Asians were 50 times and Afro-Caribbeans 36 times more liable to victimisation than white people. The failure to appreciate the seriousness of the problem has been largely due to a lack of reliable information about it. Records of racist attacks are normally kept by the police, however information on them is published in differing levels of detail. In Greater London, where the problem is more acute, more detail has been supplied. Detailed records of the arrest rate are only kept by Tower Hamlets and Ealing. However, no detailed records are kept of conviction rates or the attitude of the courts.

Police records of the nature and number of attacks are often at variance with those maintained by community groups. For example, in Tower Hamlets 277 incidents were reported to the police but the local police monitoring group dealt with 495 in 1985. The police claim that, generally, on investigation the majority of reported incidents do not contain racist motivation.

Black community organisations argue that the police persistently downgrade cases of actual bodily harm to common assault and down-grade racist incidents to neighbourhood disputes. The report also underlines the view of community organisations that the police fail to follow up enquiries into racially motivated attacks as they are basically hostile to the Black population. The report also criticises police discourtesy when a racist attack is reported, adding that Black members of the community mistrust and are intimidated by the complaints procedure.

(adapted from *Policing London*, no. 30, December 1987)

Source C

Law Report

Court of Appeal
Alexander v Home Office
Before Lord Justice May and Mr Justice Ewbank
February 12 1988

The facts

The plaintiff was of West Indian origin, serving a sentence at Parkhurst Prison. When his applications to work in the prison kitchen were rejected he began an action claiming that he had been racially discriminated against.

Judge Whitley, sitting at Southampton county court, saw two prison reports stating that the plaintiff "displays the usual traits associated with people of his ethnic background, being arrogant, suspicious of staff, anti-authority, devious..." and "shows the anti-authoritarian arrogance that seems to be common in most coloured inmates"

The judge held that the plaintiff had been treated not as an individual but as a racial stereotype, and that he had suffered racial discrimination. He awarded the plaintiff special damages, based on the difference between the higher pay in the kitchen and his actual pay.

(from the *Guardian*, 17 February 1988)

Q Data-response questions

1 Using Source A:
   (a) How have white people shown their hostility to Annette's relationship with Jerry?
   (b) What example is given in the source of 'petty apartheid?'
2 Using Source B:
   (a) Why has the seriousness of racial attacks not been fully recognised?
   (b) Why do you think that the number of racial incidents reported to the police is generally lower than the number reported to community groups?
   (c) What claim do the police make about many 'racist incidents'?
3 From Source C, what was the racial stereotype from which the West Indian prisoner suffered?
4 How would you define racism and racial discrimination?

D Discussion

What do you think are the causes of racism?

R Research suggestion

Hypothesis: Young people are less racially prejudiced than older people.
Method: Prepare a questionnaire for samples of different age groups.

Ethnic minorities in the police and civil service

Source A

Black PC who said 'Join us' quits the force

by KIM SENGUPTA

A BLACK policeman who took part in a video to attract more ethnic recruits says he has been forced to quit by racism.

Dennis Edgehill says he was asked to leave the force after being told he was "too nice".

But he claimed: "I have little doubt that that my colour was the main reason I was forced to go. There really is a strong feeling against accepting black people as policemen despite all the glossy adverts they come out with."

Mr Edgehill was a probationary officer based at Tottenham, north London. During the two years of probation a recruit can be dismissed at any time if senior officers feel he will not make a good officer.

The 28-year-old PC, who says he got good marks in exams, said racist remarks by fellow officers were commonplace.

He was once disciplined for being late. But Mr Edgehill claimed he was asked to resign with the reason: "You're too nice to be a policeman – we're not in the business of employing nice people."

Mr Edgehill, who has two A-levels, appears in uniform in the recruitment video A Force with a Future, in which he urges fellow blacks to follow his example.

Dedication

But he said yesterday: "I know better now. The job might give the impression it is bending over backwards to recruit black policemen, but it is absolute gibberish."

Senior officers at Tottenham said that Mr Edgehill simply did not have the right personality and dedication to be a policeman.

A Scotland Yard spokesman said: "The PC in question resigned voluntarily for reasons which are confidential. We totally reject any suggestions that our ethnic recruiting is for cosmetic reasons.

"We accept some officers do make racial remarks, as happens in all spheres of society. When this is discovered we take disciplinary action."

(from *Today*, 2 June 1987)

Source B: An advertisement from the civil service's 1987 ethnic minority recruitment campaign

"The Civil Service provides resources, flexibility and a sharing management structure: it gave me the best opportunity for an interesting and rewarding career."

Usha Tripathi, Curator, British Library

If you would like to know more about professional opportunities in the Civil Service, please send your name, address and brief details of areas of work in which you are interested to: Civil Service Commission, Alencon Link, Basingstoke, Hants RG21 1JB, or telephone Basingstoke (0256) 468551 (answering service operates outside office hours).

The Civil Service is an equal opportunity employer

Source C

Sikh girl who battled to join force walks the beat with pride

Shindo: The new face of the police

SHINDO BARQUER is brown, beautiful, and proud to be a policewoman.

The 21-year-old daughter of a Sikh represents the new face of Britain's police, as a determined drive continues to recruit among young blacks and Asians.

Yesterday, stepping out in uniform for the first time as a member of the West Midlands force, Shindo told how she fought against the odds to fulfil her ambition.

For the last three years, she worked in local government on a youth training programme, but never let her dream die.

'I always wanted to be a policewoman' she said. 'I even served a year as a special constable to make sure I was serious about it.'

But she discovered that getting into the full-time force is not easy. Last year, out of more than 1,000 inquiries from members of minority communities, only 38 applicants were enrolled.

By AUBREY CHALMERS

Shindo failed the entrance exam first time, but passed after taking a special course to improve her results.

However, her parents, who came from the Punjab to make their home in Warley, West Midlands, had reservations about her joining.

'They were worried about the dangerous side of the job, but it does not concern me.' she said.

And Shindo does not expect to be alienated from her community. 'My friends were a bit shocked when I was chosen, but they are still my friends,' she said. 'Nobody has turned against me.

'I will go wherever I am posted, not necessarily in black communities. I want to get as much experience as possible.'

The West Midlands force has 135 black or Asian officers — two per cent. of its strength — giving it Britain's highest proportion of ethnic minority recruits.

In England and Wales there are 935 ethnic officers out of a total strength of 122,236.

'My community isn't going to turn against me'

SHINDO... 'I was determined to join'

(from the *Daily Mail*, 14 May 1987)

Data-response questions

1 Using Sources A and C:
  (a) Give figures to show the proportion of police officers from ethnic minorities.
  (b) How have the police been trying to recruit more black officers?
  (c) What sort of problems have Shindo Barquer and Dennis Edgehill had to face in following their police careers?
2 Using Source B, what is meant by the phrase 'an equal opportunity employer'?

Discussion

Why is the government trying to recruit more black men and women into (a) the police; (b) the civil service?

Research suggestion

Hypothesis: Black people are portrayed in a stereotyped way on television.
Methods: Examine the roles given to black people on television. Prepare questionnaires for a cross-section of people asking about their views on the portrayal of black people on television.

Opportunities and the future

Source **A**: The experiences of Asian students

Krutika Tanna was born in Kenya and went to primary school in India. At the age of ten she came to live in Britain. She went to a comprehensive school in Brent where the majority of pupils were of Asian or Afro-Caribbean origin, but the staff were all white. All the Asians were put in the CSE stream but her father paid for her to be 'double-entered' so that she could take O-levels. She was given no encouragement to apply for university but she took a degree in Education and Psychology at Lancaster and then did the research for her doctorate at Aston University. She now works for the Commission for Racial Equality.

The aim of the research
In 1987 Krutika Tanna completed her research which compared the experiences of two groups of university students: White British and South Asian (whose families originated from countries such as India, Pakistan, Sri Lanka and Bangladesh).

The research methods
1 Postal questionnaires were completed by 301 South Asian and White British undergraduates from 12 universities, who were in their final year of study in 1985.
2 In-depth interviews were conducted with 49 students from the original sample.
3 Other respondents completed a second postal questionnaire and some filled in diary report forms.

The findings
1 *Before university* Both groups had similar A-level qualifications but many of the South Asian students had experienced greater difficulty in getting to university. Some had confronted racist attitudes and behaviour from both pupils and teachers. They were more likely than the White British to have:
 – been entered for CSEs rather than O-Levels,
 – taken some of their O-Levels in the Sixth Form,
 – retaken their A-Levels.
2 *At university* Some South Asians had faced academic and social difficulties due to racism. Many had felt increasingly aware of their 'Asianness' and had been drawn towards their 'cultural background' since going to university.
3 *Plans for the future* South Asian students were more likely to opt for further study after getting their degree. This was because they believed that they needed to be better qualified than their White British counterparts.

Those who were searching for work:
 – had better qualifications,
 – were willing to accept a lower salary,
 – had started applying for jobs earlier,
 – and had made more applications than the White British.

Whilst having no difficulty getting interviews, South Asian applicants were less likely to be offered employment. Many of them hoped to be self-employed eventually.

(adapted from an unpublished doctoral thesis by Krutika D. Tanna, the University of Aston in Birmingham, 1987)

Source B: Percentage of husbands and wives married to white persons, by ethnic group and age, 1984–86

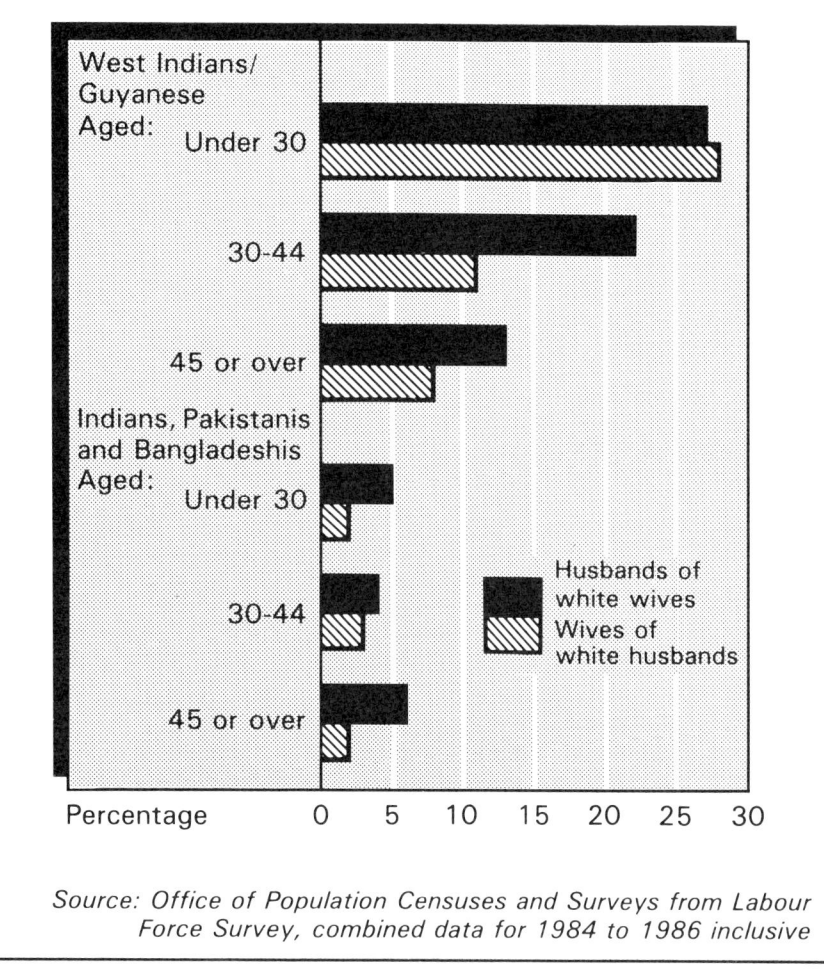

[Bar chart showing percentages of husbands of white wives and wives of white husbands, by ethnic group (West Indians/Guyanese and Indians, Pakistanis and Bangladeshis) and age (Under 30, 30–44, 45 or over). Percentage scale 0 to 30.]

Source: Office of Population Censuses and Surveys from Labour Force Survey, combined data for 1984 to 1986 inclusive

(from *Social Trends*, 1988)

Source C: 'A view of Black Britain'

Perhaps the future will see the descendants of West Indians growing more and more like Jews, our invisible immigrants. A proportion of Jews, though born in England, have customs and appearances that seem utterly strange to most English people. These are the Orthodox and intensely religious. So, among coloured people, both Rastas and some of the stranger Pentecostalist Church members, those who wear robes and turbans, may continue to practise customs that most ordinary people of all colours can only guess at. But, as among Jews, these will become very much a minority.

As among Jews, I predict, there will be thousands of coloured people who will seem entirely English. When you get to know them better, however, and enter their houses, you will find they have a few intriguing and unusual customs, forms of speech, styles of decoration and dishes of food. This helps to make the world a more delightful place to live in. And, as among Jews now, and increasingly among coloured people, there are those who seem so completely English that no-one thinks of them as anything else. I predict that among the descendants of West Indians, this may be the largest group.

(adapted from *Real Wicked, Guy: A View of Black Britain* by Roy Kerridge, Basil Blackwell, 1983)

D Discussion

What conclusions would you draw from the above sources regarding the relations between ethnic groups in Britain in the future?

7 Education

The curriculum

Source A: One view of what we learn in school

Now I've left school and faced the 'big wide world' I can look back at the subjects I did in school, see how they've helped me, and suggest some changes.

PE: I think us females should be taught more about the most popular games (football and cricket) so we can understand them better when watching TV or reading the newspaper.

Geography: This was an example of a subject being too scientific. My lessons consisted of things like learning about soil: why Cornwall was marshy and London used to be but isn't now. I would love to know more about the people in different countries.

Maths: So many of the subjects like calculus I will never use again, whereas adding, takeaways, percentages and so on weren't covered enough.

Cookery: A lot of it was about baking cakes. I never learnt how to cook a proper three-course meal, or cope with a weekly menu. It would have helped to know about the ideal things to eat at break times when you started work.

Woodwork: I never learnt how to put up a shelf or how to make a small cupboard. I can remember once being told to make a 'freaky' sculpture to stick a candle in. What use is that to me?

English: I think pupils would be just as interested in how books and newspapers are made as in the stories that go into them.

History: I would like to know more about the subjects that were a reality for millions of people – like World War II, or why Russia went Communist.

Music: Music lessons could open a door to the reality of to-day's music industry by teaching about synthesisers, recording studios, how a record is put together, as well as old-fashioned things like classical music and instruments.

Driving: I reckon half the people that left school at the same time as me have a car or are intending to buy one. School could tell you how to go about this as well as the Highway Code, tax and insurance and the basics of driving and car maintenance.

Money: Perhaps pupils should know why they find that their parents cannot afford 'luxury' items – because they've got the gas bill, the electricity bill and they're paying for the house. How do you get a mortgage? How do banks work out their interest?

(by Ley Alberici, aged 17, Great Barr, Birmingham, from *Tales Out Of School* by Roger White and David Brockington, Routledge & Kegan Paul, 1983)

Source B: School rules for pupils in the USSR

1 Master the foundations of science and the skills of self-education with determination and perseverance.
2 Take an active part in socially useful labour. Prepare yourself for the conscious choice of a job. In doing labour tasks, strictly observe safety rules.
3 Take an active part in the social and cultural life of your school, town, village and the work of the pupil self-government committees.
4 Concern yourself with the protection and growth of the national wealth, the riches of nature.
5 Systematically practise physical culture and sport. Strengthen yourself. Prepare yourself for the defence of the Soviet Motherland.
6 Master modern culture and technology. Develop your skills in different fields of activity.
7 Plan and use your time sensibly. Be punctual. Learn how to organize your work correctly.
8 Live according to the norms of the socialist community. Be a worthy example of good behaviour to your younger comrades. Be intolerant towards amoral and anti-social activities.
9 Help to strengthen the school collective, preserve and develop its useful traditions. Be a principled and honourable comrade.
10 Respect your parents. Show a constant regard for all members of the family. Help with the housework.
11 Respect your teachers' work. Carry out and actively support the teachers' requests and the decisions of the organs of pupil self-government.

(from *Soviet Economy and Society* by D. Lane, Basil Blackwell, 1985)

Education

Source C

(from the *Guardian*, 17 February 1988)

Why we really like school

SCHOOL'S IN! — that's the main finding of the latest Young Guardian/Carrick James Opinion Poll. But while our sample expressed reasonable sympathy for the teachers over pay and conditions, a majority (54 per cent) believed their education had been affected as a result of strikes and other teacher protests. A third complained they were subject to bullying at school and said they did not like going for that reason.

We asked a representative sample* of 10 — 17-year-olds in Great Britain (not Northern Ireland) what they thought of school, the subjects they took, and of the teachers and how recent strikes and other disruptions had affected them.

Of going to school 20 per cent said they enjoyed it very much while 44 per cent said they liked, or quite liked, it. A further 20 per cent had no feeling either way. Only 3 per cent said they hated it (out of 12 per cent who didn't like it in one way or another).

But girls like it more than boys — 67 per cent of girls overall expressed some like, compared with 59 per cent of boys.

When we asked what three things our sample liked, most of the boys listed sport (almost three-quarters named this) as top, followed by seeing or playing with friends and then doing particular subjects. The girls also liked sports — but that came third (49 per cent) behind friends (listed by 57 per cent) and then certain lessons or subjects (50 per cent).

School seems, then, to be a place you go for the social side — mixing with friends and playing games and sport — although learning is another important aspect.

This is borne out by other answers. For instance, we asked in more general terms what our sample liked about school. Overall, 53 per cent said it was a friendly place; 75 per cent liked seeing or playing with friends. Nearly half (47 per cent) liked the teachers.

There are some strong dislikes. Slightly more than half (54 per cent) did not like the teachers (presumably one per cent are just confused). Nearly three fifths (57 per cent) did not like some subjects, while a quarter thought it a noisy place where people shouted a lot.

More ominously, 12 per cent said it was a rough place where there were a lot of fights. Nearly a third said they were bullied. It will come as no surprise to know that nearly a half disliked going because they had to get up too early (47 per cent).

Looking at the subject likes and dislikes, the breakdown was:

Subject	Liked Girls	Liked Boys	Disliked Girls	Disliked Boys
Maths	40	47	29	25
English	50	46	16	20
Science	33	41	21	13
Computing	27	33	6	2
Foreign languages	28	18	18	22
Sports/games	55	69	13	6
Religious subjects	14	11	20	24
History	25	28	16	17
Geography	23	31	23	17
Music	34	20	12	20
Art	49	44	6	10
Practical subjects	36	44	5	6

We also asked about attitudes to teachers. Overall, 70 per cent of the sample thought they were helpful, a further 19 per cent being unsure; only seven per cent thought they did not. they were good to have a laugh with.

Intriguingly, 69 per cent did not think their class too large (around a quarter of the sample said they were in a class of 30, a further 13 per cent in one with 25/26). Two fifths thought teachers were in a reasonably well paid job, a fifth thought they were not.

We asked the same question the other way round (ie they are not paid enough — true, between, untrue?) and got comparable results. In this case 47 per cent said the statement was untrue, a quarter said they were not paid enough. 54 per cent had been affected or bothered by the disruptions and strikes among teachers.

Over three fifths said teachers had a grievance. 37 per cent said only a few, 28 per cent said they had none. The grievances, they thought, came down mainly to pay, although 10 per cent said unruly behaviour by pupils was the reason. Half expressed little or no sympathy for these grievances, while 44 per cent were fairly sympathetic.

But when we asked if they controlled their classes there was an even split between a third who thought they did, slightly less who were not sure and the 34 per cent who thought they did not. Around a quarter thought teachers were too soft while two fifths thought that "untrue". Nearly two thirds said some teachers got cross while nearly four fifths thought

* *The Young Guardian/Carrick James Survey was a representative quota sample of 631 10-17 year olds interviewed in the home in December, 1987 throughout Great Britain.*

Q Data-response questions

1 Using Source A:
  (a) Chose two of the suggestions for changing subjects and explain why you agree or disagree with them.
  (b) Which subjects should be compulsory, core subjects in a National Curriculum for all fourteen- and fifteen-year olds? Give a full explanation.

2 Using Source B:
  (a) Describe the kind of person that these rules are designed to produce.
  (b) What is the 'hidden curriculum'? Give three examples of what pupils are meant to learn from it.

3 Using Source C:
  (a) Describe the sample used in this study.
  (b) What percentage of those surveyed said that they liked or quite liked school?
  (c) What differences were found between the reasons why boys liked school and the reasons why girls liked school?
  (d) Which classroom subject was most liked by boys and which was most liked by girls?
  (e) Is there any evidence in the table in Source C of sex-role stereotyping? Use figures to support your answer.

D Discussion

What would you lay down as the most important ten rules for an effective secondary school?

R Research suggestion

Test some of the findings mentioned in Source C by carrying out a survey in your school.

Schools do matter

The myth exploded: schools really do matter

In maths, school has 10 times the influence of home

This morning, one of the great post-war educational myths is demolished for ever. For nearly 20 years, the belief that children's home backgrounds are of far greater importance than the schools they attend has dominated educational thinking. Good results have been attributed to favoured school intakes, poor results to social disadvantages.

Now a new study shows that schools do matter. It demonstrates that junior schools can affect children's progress to such an extent that the best and the worst schools can reverse the long-established advantage of middle-class over working-class children.

The study is by a team, led by Professor Peter Mortimore, which traced the fortunes of 2,000 children in 50 London schools over the four years (seven to eleven) of junior schooling.

It must be emphasized that the study confirms the decisive influence of home background on attainment. At seven, children whose parents worked in non-manual jobs were nearly 10 months further ahead in reading than pupils from unskilled manual homes. By the end of the third year, the gap had widened.

At seven those with non-manual fathers wrote stories with an average length of 110 words; those with fathers in unskilled work averaged 73 words. Again the gap widened during junior school.

Dozens of other studies have concluded that social class determines attainment far more than any influence of particular schools. According to Professor Mortimore, these other studies have missed two crucial points: first, average differences between social classes may obscure how individual children perform in individual schools. Second, though *attainment* throughout schooling may be heavily influenced by social class, because children start from such different points, *progress* is another matter.

Suppose that one seven-year-old has a score of 50 on a maths test, the other 75. By 11, the first child has increased her score to 70, the other to 80. The second child's attainment remains higher, but her progress has clearly been slower. It is this kind of difference that Professor Mortimore examined.

And he found that schools have an overwhelming influence on children's progress between 7 and 11. One school raised average reading performance by 24 per cent, maths scores by 21 per cent, writing quality by 15 per cent. Another school depressed scores to almost exactly the same extent.

The researchers analysed the social classes in 21 schools. In the three most effective, working-class children averaged higher reading scores than middle-class children in the four least effective.

So what made some schools better than others? 'It is the factors within the control of the head and teachers that are crucial,' the authors say. They identified 12 ways in which a junior school can make itself more effective (see box).

Education

Birth dates count

THE study shows that school success is influenced by date of birth. At seven, a child born in the autumn term averaged 51.4 on a reading test, while a summer-born child averaged 40.8. There were similar disparities in maths and writing tests. The differences were unchanged by the end of junior school.

Summer children were nearly twice as likely to have behaviour difficulties and more likely to have negative attitudes to school. Some studies suggest that such problems — created by being the youngest in their classes — persist throughout secondary school and even beyond.

Twelve factors which make a good primary school

THE study identifies 12 key factors that make a good junior school:
- A head who leads his staff without exerting total control.
- An established deputy head, who is rarely absent and to whom the head delegates important duties.
- Teachers are given a say in such matters as spending and curriculum planning.
- Consistency between teachers in their approach to learning.
- Encouraging children to manage their own work, but not giving them complete freedom to choose what they do.
- Intellectually stimulating talk between children and teachers, involving challenging questions; telling the children what to do without explaining its purpose is less effective.
- Creating work-centred classrooms, where the noise level is low and teachers are able to discuss the content of learning with children, rather than spending time on routine matters.
- Lessons that concentrate on one subject (or, at most, two subjects) rather than mixing three or more curriculum areas.
- Pupil's work should be geared to the ability of the individual child.
- Maximum communication between the teacher and the whole class, but not traditional chalk-and-talk.
- Keeping written records of pupils' work and progress.
- Parental involvement in classrooms, school visits and in helping children at home. Formal parent-teacher associations, however, were ineffective.
- Emphasis on praising and rewarding, rather than punishing and criticising children.

Lessons in one subject are the best, the report says

(from the *Independent*, 24 March 1988)

Q Data-response questions

(a) What educational myth, according to the writer, has been dismissed?
(b) According to the writer, how has the new study demolished this myth?
(c) How did Peter Mortimore conduct his study?
(d) What was his conclusion about the effect of home background on educational achievement?
(e) What two points, according to Peter Mortimore, have previous studies missed and failed to explain?
(f) Which of the twelve factors which make a good primary school do you think are the most important and the least important?
(g) Describe how three aspects of home background might have an important effect on the educational performance of pupils.

D Discussion

What do you think are the most important factors making for an effective secondary school?

R Research suggestion

Hypothesis: There is little agreement about what makes a person an effective teacher.
Method: Give a questionnaire to a random sample of pupils and to a random sample of teachers. Conduct in-depth interviews with a number of pupils and with a number of teachers.

Private education

Source A

THE "hidden curriculum" which independent schools are said to provide is in the news again (Guardian, January 12, quoting the new Chairman of the Incorporated Association of Preparatory Schools). I wonder which module in that curriculum prompted a boorish sixth form boy from an independent school to make a most insulting comment to a group of students from a Hertfordshire comprehensive last week?

Sixteen of my A level students had spent a very enjoyable and stimulating day at King's College, London, attending lectures and seminars for A level students of English and their teachers. A group of them (all, I might add, committed, studious, well-behaved, and very "presentable") were about to enter a lift when the odious youth turned to say, "Oh, we don't want the Grange Hill mob!" There was no teacher present, of course, which is just as well, because had I been there, I think I would have done him an injury.

An adult might simply dismiss such loutish behaviour, but one of the girls to whom this remark was addressed told me afterwards that she felt "common, cheapened, and put down." It spoiled the day for them and ruined the atmosphere. These students are going on to university and polytechnic — should they expect more of the same in higher education?

Another of our students, at a "good" university (not Oxbridge) was taunted by independent school products as "comprehensive trash." How to be patronising/downright insulting to the lower orders, to keep them in their place, is obviously part of the hidden curriculum.

What are the staff at such schools doing to change the attitudes of their pupils? And perhaps themselves? Or is something so deeply entrenched impossible to change?

The position could well deteriorate further. The attitude of this Government towards state education has been such that prejudice, rooted as always in ignorance, finds fertile soil in the minds of independent school pupils and their parents. Purchased privilege ensures that the purchaser thinks he/she is getting a superior product — at the price of a divided society.

No wonder some of us think that all the while the public schools exist we shall never get things right in this country

Catherine Henderson (Mrs).
24 Mandeville Road,
Hertford.

(a letter to the *Guardian*, 26 January 1988)

Source B: Two replies to Source A

A curriculum that should stay hidden

IT WAS with interest but no surprise, that I read Catherine Henderson's letter (Education Guardian, January 26) referring to a certain aspect of the "hidden curriculum" of independent schools.

Although we could easily have afforded to send our children to independent schools, my husband and I decided to stick to our principles and have them educated entirely in the state sector. We have never had cause to regret that decision.

In general, we have been very satisfied with the education they have received. In particular, we have been especially grateful for the friends they have made in state schools up and down the country.

Some years ago, we were moved to live in the south of England for a few years. One evening, soon after our arrival, I overheard a conversation between my younger daughter, then aged eight, and the even younger boy next door, the privileged pupil of an expensive local prep school.

"What time do you leave school in the afternoon?" he demanded. "Three-thirty," she replied innocently. "Huh," was the scornful retort, "we finish at five o'clock, not like 'common muck' such as you."

Happily my daughter, unlike Mrs Henderson's sensitive sixth-formers, did not feel at all cheapened or put down. She simply remarked to us later, how glad she was that we did not make her attend the same school as such a rude and unpleasant child.

One would not expect a "hidden" curriculum to have had time to take effect on a child of seven and one would feel inclined to blame the parents.

However, this boy's parents were always friendly and polite to all our family.

It seems to me that many independent schools do not make much effort to "hide" this part of their curriculum.

I was very tempted to ring the headmaster with some suggestion as to what he might do with the extra one and a half hours in school.

"Common parent."
(Name and address supplied).

I READ, with astonishment, Mrs Henderson's sweeping generalisations about the public school system — an attack seemingly brought on by the behaviour of *one* boorish boy (Education Guardian, January 26). Is she really saying that all pupils attending comprehensive schools are models of good manners and courteous behaviour?

My daughter attended state primary schools until the age of 11 and I was extremely happy with her progress and impressed by the standard of education she received. I was a teacher in such a school.

However, when she reached 11 we chose to send her to an independent school with an excellent reputation, for the simple reason that we felt our local comprehensive school would not provide her with an education suitable to her needs. She is academically bright and we felt the only state school available to her did little to encourage gifted children.

Even more important, judging by the many children we know who attend there, it does not encourage good manners and courtesy, or discipline the children in a way which we feel is essential.

Unlike Mrs Henderson, this does not lead me to the opinion that all comprehensive schools are bad. We would have been happy to have sent our child to a good state school. Surely any intelligent, unbiased person must know that there are good and bad schools in both private and state sectors, and that all schools contain some ill-mannered children?

By her remarks, Mrs Henderson is being as insulting and biased towards the pupils and staff of independent schools as that ignorant young man was towards her sixth-form pupils.

Astonished.
(Name and address supplied).

(from the *Guardian*, 2 February 1988)

Education

Source C: A Cabinet's privilege

Fifteen of the twenty-one cabinet members of the Conservative government in April 1988 went to fee-paying private schools:

School (1988 fees before extras in brackets)	Ministers who attended
Eton (£6,450)	Douglas Hurd, Nicholas Ridley, Paul Channon, Lord Belstead
Winchester (£6,690)	Sir Geoffrey Howe, Nigel Lawson, George Younger
George Heriot's (£6,480)	Lord Mackay
Latymer (£2,775)	Peter Walker
Rugby (£6,750)	Tom King
St Pauls (£5,928)	Kenneth Baker
Nottingham High (£6,080)	Kenneth Clarke
Merchiston Castle (£5,970)	John MacGregor
George Watson's (£4,476)	Malcolm Rifkind
Charterhouse (£7,116)	John Wakeham

Only three of the twenty-two in the Labour Shadow Cabinet of April 1988 went to fee-paying schools:

Berkhamsted (£5,310)	Michael Meacher
Glasgow Academy (£2,115)	Donald Dewar
Bryanston (£2,300)	Lord Ponsonby

Data-response questions

1 Using Source B:
   (a) Why did the writer of the first letter not send his/her children to an independent school?
   (b) What principles do you think are being referred to?
   (c) The writer of the first letter says that 'independent schools do not make much of an effort to "hide" this part of their curriculum'. What part of the curriculum is the writer referring to?
   (d) What suggestion do you think the writer would make to the headmaster regarding the extra one and a half hours that are spent in the independent school by the pupils?
   (e) Why did the writer of the second letter not send his/her daughter to the local state school?
2 What are the strengths and weaknesses of the type of evidence contained in Sources A and B?
3 Why is Source C called 'A Cabinet's privilege'?

Discussion

'The quality of education provided by public schools is shown by the high percentage of top jobs occupied by ex-public school pupils.'

Research suggestion

Hypothesis: Most parents are satisfied with the standard of education that their children receive in state schools.
Method: Give a questionnaire to a random sample of parents. Pupils could take the questionnaire home for their parents to fill in. The questionnaire could perhaps contain the question, 'Would you send your child or children to an independent school if you could afford it?'.

8 Social stratification

Two types of stratification

Source **A:** Gender stratification

Clear the rails of prejudice, demand women

Tom Stoddart

It's her line:
Dyan Wood, who runs 10 stations in the west Croydon area, overcame hostility from the men she manages by 'showing I could do the job'

PATRICIA ROCHE, a female train driver, was nearly sacked by her male superiors for being "too weak" to couple up a train to a carriage quickly enough.

Luckily, she survived; for her departure would have severely depleted the ranks of one of the most exclusive groups in the world: the 17 out of British Rail's 19,300 train drivers who are women.

The pressure put on Roche was nothing unusual — all her colleagues have their own stories of sexual discrimination on the railways. Three others who would have boosted the numbers have been forced to resign, she claims, because of the catalogue of sexism they faced: barriers to promotion, verbal harassment and physical abuse, ranging from being sexually assaulted to having pornographic magazines thrust in their faces.

BR's record on employment of women was so bad that a report from the Equal Opportunities Commission nearly two years ago demanded an end to practices which exclude women from the industry and make the lives of those who do get in a misery.

Despite that, however, female employees last week said that little has changed: BR and the rail unions are still operating what is virtually a closed shop for men.

Even though BR set up an equal-opportunities unit two years ago, the women dismissed moves to stamp out the problems since the June 1986 commission report as "cosmetic".

They said little had been done to encourage women to apply for work such as driving trains. Once in such jobs, managers and union officials allowed widespread abuse and ignored complaints about harassment. The most common discriminatory practices involve:

● **Outdated attitudes.** Managers and union officials, for example, still believe driving a train involves "heavy and arduous" work that women could not do, or would not like to do. Women thinking of becoming train drivers are put off by such attitudes.

One senior BR spokesman last week told The Sunday Times that the job did not appeal to women because it was too "physically exerting" getting down from locomotives when parked at depots. Women drivers dismissed that as ridiculous.

● **Male networks.** Vacancies are often advertised by word of mouth, from man to man, father to son. Often a woman is deliberately ignored or picked on by her male colleagues in a bid to make her quit, with nothing being done by union representatives or managers to end it.

● **Restrictive union practices.** Long-established customs and agreements favour continued male domination. These include deals allowing promotion only on the number of years served. Such a strict seniority system means all the best-paid jobs, such as drivers on inter-city routes, go to men.

Only 9,000 of BR's 139,000 employees are female — mostly in clerical jobs. Like drivers, most guards and station managers are men. Out of more than 10,000 guards, 89 are female. There are just 30 women station managers or area supervisors, compared to 5,340 men.

(from *The Sunday Times*, 13 March 1988)

Social stratification

Source B: Ethnic stratification

Ethnic minorities have double the white unemployment rate

Christopher Huhne
Economics Editor

PEOPLE from the ethnic minorities are twice as likely to be unemployed as white men and women, according to figures published yesterday.

An analysis of figures by the Department of Employment shows that 32 per cent of 16 to 24-year-old men from the ethnic minorities are out of work, compared to 18 per cent of white men in the same age group.

Among those of West Indian and Pakistani origin, the rate is said to be 37 per cent.

The figures are based on an average of the Department of Employment Gazette's three labour force surveys, published between 1984 and 1986. Although unemployment has fallen sharply since then, relative figures are unlikely to have changed.

The position for young women is almost as bad: some 31 per cent of young women from the ethnic minorities are unemployed, against 15 per cent for young white women.

The picture for all ages and sexes shows that ethnic unemployment is exactly double white unemployment — 20 per cent against 10 per cent.

The hardest-hit are those of Pakistani and Bangladeshi origin, with a 31 per cent unemployment rate against 22 per cent for those of West Indian and Guyanese origin and 16 per cent for those of Indian origin.

Other conclusions include:
● Around 4.6 per cent of the population of working age — roughly 1.5 million people — are from the ethnic minorities. Of these, 489,000 are of Indian origin, 375,000 of West Indian or Guyanese, and 269,000 of Pakistani or Bangladeshi.
● The proportion of the total population belonging to ethnic minorities is likely to increase because they already comprise 7.5 per cent of those under 16.
● The proportion of self-employed people among the ethnic minorities is 24 per cent for Indians and 22 per cent for those of Pakistani and Bangladeshi origin, against 14 per cent overall.
● People from the ethnic minorities account for more than 6 per cent of the working population in Greater London and the west Midlands metropolitan county.

(from the *Guardian*, 10 March 1988)

Data-response questions

1 Using Source A:
   (a) Which group is referred to as the most exclusive group in the world?
   (b) What were the reasons why, according to Patricia Roche, three female train drivers resigned?
   (c) Describe two discriminatory practices which prevent women from applying for work such as driving trains.
   (d) What could be done to make British Rail a less sexist organisation?
2 Using Source B, which ethnic group has the highest unemployment rate?
3 Describe one area other than employment in which members of particular ethnic groups experience prejudice and discrimination.
4 Explain the meaning of the term 'stratification.'

Discussion

Do the career ambitions of your friends show that traditional gender roles are breaking down?

Research suggestion

Carry out a piece of historical research into a stratification system of the past. Present an examination of the main groups and the relations between them as well as an account of any changes that affected or brought about the end of the stratification system.

Aspects of class in Britain

Source A: Class and education

Britain is notorious for its class divisions. But most of us assume that the gaps are closing, and that we have been evolving into a more classless society.

When BBC2's '40 Minutes' set up an exchange last summer between 10 first-year sixth formers from Rugby, the £6,750-a-year public school, and 10 from Ruffwood, an admired comprehensive in Kirkby on the edge of Liverpool, we expected it would show how far British society has progressed towards that ideal.

How wrong we were! We knew that each group would find the manners, speech and surroundings of the other alien. What was disturbing about the fortnight was that there was no real meeting of minds. I detected depressingly little evidence of shared values or feelings.

They were all bright, highly educated young people. They read the same literature and are trained in broadly similar subjects. But during the exchange they might have belonged to two different races.

Rugbeians call anyone who has a bit of an accent or wears white socks 'Kevin'. The female of 'Kevin' is 'Sharon'. This is applied not only to outsiders, but also to scholarship boys who go to Rugby from less well-off families.

They were all on their best behaviour when they showed the Ruffwood sixth-formers round their school one Sunday afternoon last May. Accents, hair styles, clothes and shoes and everything about the visitors showed that they were 'Kevins' and 'Sharons'. But they were received with courtesy. Everyone wanted the fortnight to be a success. Both groups were friendly and likeable kids.

The politeness remained, but both sides were deeply unsettled by parts of the experience. The Ruffwood visitors found most Rugby schoolboys arrogant. Their Rugby hosts often seemed uninterested in them. Disappointed, the Ruffwood students felt crushed and humiliated. Their response was often sullen silence.

Later in the week, as they found the going easier, they became openly critical: of the regimentation at Rugby ('a remand centre for the rich'), of the readiness of Rugby parents to forsake the company of their children for so much of their childhood, of the uncritical acceptance of authority, and of what they interpreted as lack of emotional maturity.

Many Rugby boys are intended for the army. 'They treat war as some kind of game,' said a Ruffwood boy. 'They'd love to get in there and shoot someone. They don't seem to understand how atrocious war can be.'

There was a similar sense of unease among the Rugbeians when they reached Merseyside. It emerged that one or two of the Rugby kids had never travelled on a bus before. One remarked to his Kirkby host in all seriousness: 'If it's really a 15-minute walk to school, couldn't we take a taxi?'.

Rugby students were depressed by the visual appearance of Kirkby, and sometimes seemed blind to the humanity that lies behind its unattractive appearance. One Rugbeian said that the only solution to Kirkby's problem was to drop a bomb on it.

What struck me most forcibly was not merely the absence of mutual identification, but the sheer lack of curiosity among the mentally alert youngsters of both schools. Sadly, there is a drawing back into the layers of Britain's traditional social structure.

(from 'Two nations even at school' by Chris Curling in the *Observer*, 7 February 1988)

Source B: Class and the death rate

Whatever health minister Edwina Currie may say about people in the north not eating the right food, the statistics show that health is much more dependent on class than on geographical considerations. For instance, the annual death rate for class I in the south west is 357 per 100,000 of the population, while that in the north west is 439 per 100,000 (a difference of 23%). But if classes I and V are compared in the south west the difference is a massive 167% (that is, 357 and 982 per 100,000 of the population respectively).

With more people out of work for more than a year, the number of people classified into class V is on the increase. In July 1981, 22 per cent of the unemployed had been unemployed for more than 52 weeks. Five years later this figure had almost doubled – to 41.1 per cent in July 1986. This growth in the long-term unemployed may partly explain why the incidence of suicide or self-inflicted injury in class V is twice as high as in class I.

(adapted from 'Healthy and Wealthy' in *Labour Research*, vol. 76, no. 1, January 1987)

Social stratification

Source C: Class and the infant mortality rate (1984 figures)

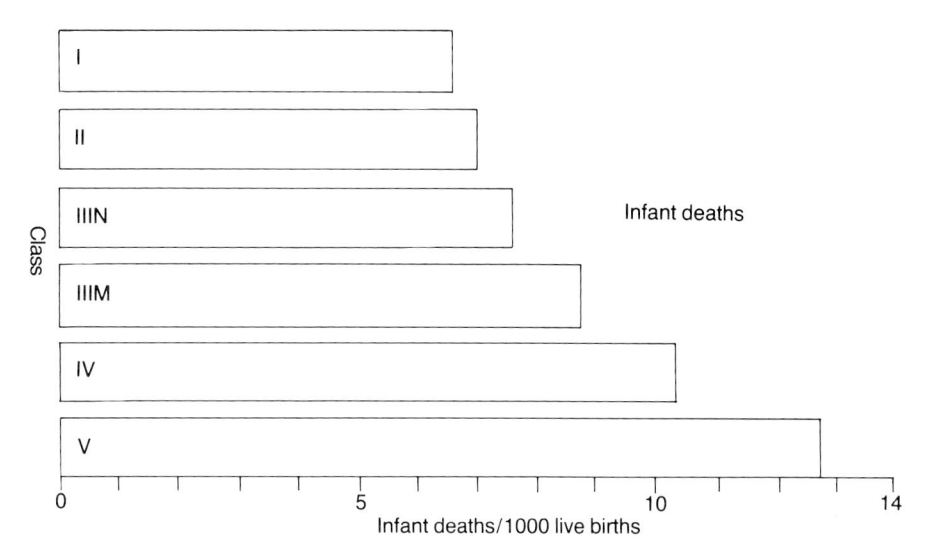

[Bar chart showing infant deaths per 1000 live births by class:
- I: ~7
- II: ~8
- IIIN: ~8
- IIIM: ~9
- IV: ~10
- V: ~13

X-axis: Infant deaths/1000 live births (0 to 14)
Y-axis: Class]

(from *The Health Divide* by M. Whitehead, Health Education Council, 1987)

Data-response questions

1. Using Source A:
   (a) Explain why the writer says, 'How wrong we were!'.
   (b) What did the two groups involved in this exchange have in common?
   (c) What did the Rugbeians mean by 'Kevins' and 'Sharons'?
   (d) Use some quotations to show the responses of members of the group from Ruffwood to Rugby and the responses of the Rugbeians to Ruffwood.
   (e) What did this exchange show about the society that we live in?
2. Using Source B:
   (a) How do 'the statistics show that health is much more dependent on class than on geographical considerations'?
   (b) Why is class V increasing?
3. Using Source C:
   (a) Use two figures to show the connection between the infant mortality rate and class.
   (b) What is meant by the term 'infant mortality rate'?
   (c) What reasons would you give for the poorer health of members of class V compared with the health of class I members?
4. What can be learned about social class in Britain today from Sources A, B and C?

Discussion

In what other areas besides health and education are class differences evident?

Research suggestion

Hypothesis: There is very little social mobility, that is, most children end up as adults occupying the same class position as their parents.
Method: Ask a sample of adults (1) what was their first full-time job, (2) what is their present job, (3) what jobs have their parents had.

Changes in the class structure

Source A: Changes in employment

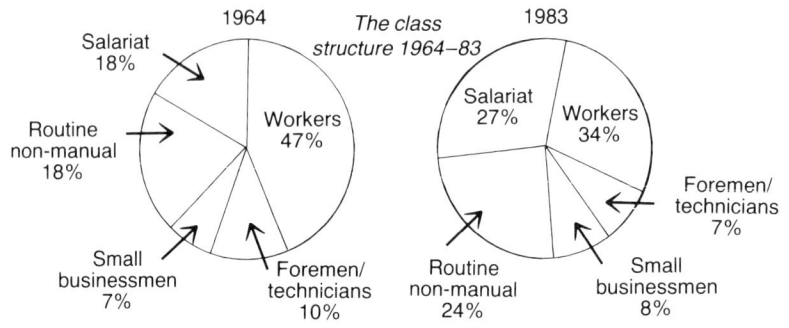

The class structure 1964–83

1964:
- Salariat 18%
- Routine non-manual 18%
- Small businessmen 7%
- Foremen/technicians 10%
- Workers 47%

1983:
- Salariat 27%
- Workers 34%
- Foremen/technicians 7%
- Small businessmen 8%
- Routine non-manual 24%

Note: The 'salariat' comprises managers, administrators, professionals and supervisors of non-manuals

(from *How Britain Votes* by Heath et al, Pergamon, 1985)

Source B: People in employment, by sex and occupation

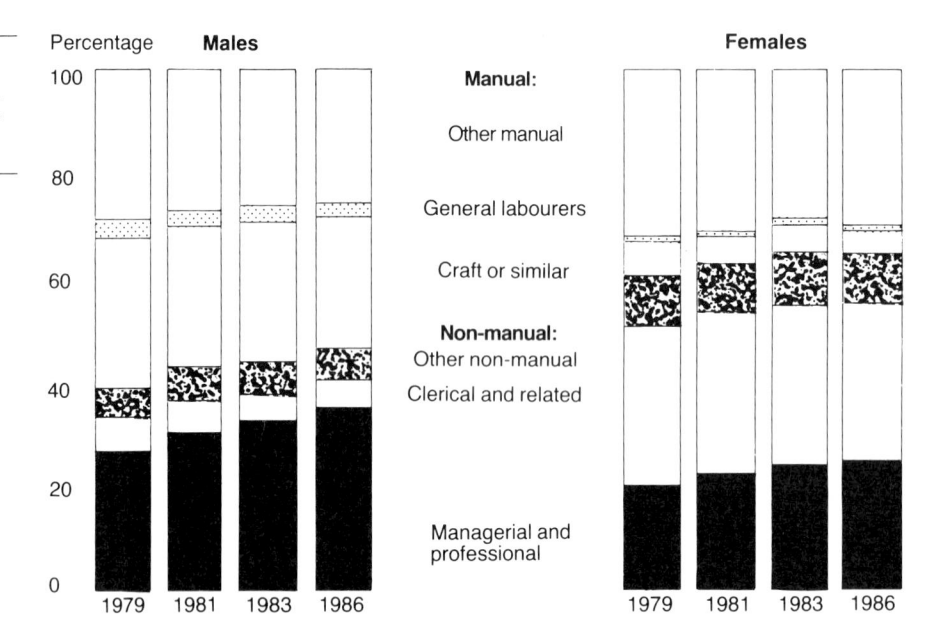

Bar charts for Males and Females, 1979, 1981, 1983, 1986, showing:

Manual:
- Other manual
- General labourers
- Craft or similar

Non-manual:
- Other non-manual
- Clerical and related
- Managerial and professional

(from *Social Trends*, 1988)

Source C: The manual service working class

People often equate the manual working class with the production industries, and white-collar workers with 'services'. The conclusion is then drawn that the growth of service employment compared with manufacturing employment involves a 'decline' in the working class. But the equation is quite misplaced. Some of the most important 'service industries' employ mainly manual workers of the traditional sort. Dustmen, hospital ancillary workers, dockers, lorry drivers, bus and train drivers, postal workers are all part of the 'service' workforce. And a very big part.... Nearly 60 per cent of all 'service' employment is covered by these categories. So manual workers are still about half the employed workforce, despite the decline in manufacturing employment....

Two occupational changes within the working class

(a) Some traditional groups of 'service' manual workers have been in decline for many years. So the number of registered dockers has shrunk massively in the last three decades from 70,000 in 1956 to about 14,000 today. There has been a somewhat smaller decline in the number of railworkers, from around 425,000 in 1951 to about 147,000 in 1985....

(b) Some groups of manual workers have grown substantially, at least until recently. For instance, the number of workers in the health service doubled between 1951 and 1974, and has continued to increase, although slowly, since. There has been a similar upward growth in areas such as hotels and catering ... and in retail distribution.

(from *The Changing Working Class* by A. Callinicos and C. Harman, Bookmarks, 1987)

Source D: Class polarisation and social mobility

It appears that a polarisation (a drawing apart) is taking place between

- the comfortable, the secure and the prosperous of the middle classes and the skilled working classes,
- various groups of outsiders, mostly weakly supplied with market capabilities, including
  - many of the young,
  - a lot of the unskilled and semi-skilled older workers,
  - a disproportionate number of black and brown Britons.

Between 1979 and 1983 the real wages of non-manual workers rose, on average, by 19 per cent, while the pay of manual workers rose by only 10 per cent.

Goldthorpe and Payne have updated the 1972 Oxford Mobility Study using data from the 1983 British General Election Survey. They note a continuing expansion of the 'service class' of non-routine white collar employees. This offers continuing opportunities for upward mobility.

At the same time the rise in unemployment between 1972 and 1983 had also led to increased chances of 'downward mobility' out of paid employment altogether. Working-class men are much more prone to this risk than other groups (between 1974 and 1984 the number of full-time male employees fell by 11 per cent while the number of part-time female employees rose by 22 per cent). In short, manual workers' chances of mobility have declined.

(adapted from *Inside British Society* by G. A. Causer, Wheatsheaf, 1987)

Data-response questions

1. Using Source A:
   (a) Which occupations are included in the category 'salariat'?
   (b) Which group has decreased most between 1964 and 1983?
2. Using Source B, how did the proportion of non-manual male and female workers alter between 1979 and 1986?
3. Using Source C:
   (a) Why is it a mistake to identify the manual working class only with production workers?
   (b) Why is it a mistake to assume that the growth of service sector jobs has led to a decline in the size of the working class?
4. Using Source D:
   (a) What does it mean if one is 'weakly supplied with capabilities' in the labour market?
   (b) What is meant by the idea of 'class polarisation'?
   (c) Why have chances of downward mobility increased while possibilities of upward mobility have continued?

Discussion

'The Labour Party has traditionally pitched its appeal at unionised, white, male, skilled manual workers in traditional industries such as mining. Such workers are now a small minority of the working class as a whole. It would be better for Labour to try to appeal (as Ken Livingstone's Labour Greater London Council did in the early 1980s) to minority groups, such as women, welfare claimants, the disabled, ethnic minorities, pensioners, gays and lesbians, because such minorities now form a majority of the modern working class.'

Research suggestion

Hypothesis: Mobility into the middle class has been widespread since 1945 and not just because of expanded educational opportunities for the working class.

Method: Interview a number of people in occupations categorised as I or II by the Registrar-General (i.e. the 'salariat' or 'service class', e.g. teachers). Find out what proportion
(a) came from working-class or junior non-manual backgrounds,
(b) used educational qualifications as a route into their present jobs.

Class in the USSR

The official view

In the early 1960s the prominent Soviet sociologist M. N. Rutkevich stated that 'The concept of "lower" and "higher" social strata is fundamentally inapplicable to Soviet socialist society. The USSR does not have higher and lower classes and strata.'

The official Soviet view is that there are two classes and one 'stratum' in the USSR. The working class and the peasantry are 'fraternal' or 'non-antagonistic' classes. Within the working class, non-manual workers ('rabotniki' or employees) are distinguished as a stratum separate from manual workers ('rabochie' or workers). The workforce in the early 1980s was divided as follows:

The working class
35 million non-manual employees (20 million with higher education)
70 million manual industrial workers
11 million agricultural workers in state farms

The peasantry
14 million agricultural workers in collective farms

The view from the West

Many Western commentators see the USSR as socially stratified into five socio-economic groups:

1 The Nomenklatura
The Nomenklatura system consists of two lists:

(a) the 'uchetnaya' are the million or so elite administrators who have been approved by the party to fill vacancies as they occur on:

(b) the 'osnovnaya' list of 600,000 key political and economic management positions.

Those in such top jobs often enjoy perks, for example:

- larger, more modern housing,
- chauffeur-driven cars,
- cheap holidays in luxury hotels,
- access to well-equipped hospitals,
- free or cheap services,
- access to special shops with Western goods and other items which are in short supply.

The children of the party bosses tend to get a privileged education in the best Moscow schools and they then gain access to some of the most attractive jobs. Brezhnev, Andropov and Gromyko are all recent top politicians whose sons obtained posts in the foreign ministry or the ministry of foreign trade. Such jobs allowed them to live in comfort, with access to Western luxuries and to postings overseas.

But the sons of the elite have avoided the more risky, more political, top jobs and so the 'new ruling class' has remained an 'open' elite. As Walker has said:

> the bright young apparatchiks (officials in the party apparatus) from outside the magic circle can still make their way to the top (Gorbachev's father was a tractor driver). This, it should be noted, is in keeping with the traditional way in which class systems have developed in Russia. Peter the Great established his post-feudal society along similar lines, allowing the traditional aristocracy to keep their lands and privileges while opening the ranks of the nobility to the bright civil servants who actually ran the state.

2 The intelligentsia
These may be broadly defined as specialists with higher education. But this highly qualified, creative, executive and technical stratum does not always receive high wages (see table in next column). Around 70 per cent of Soviet doctors and teachers are women.

Raisa Gorbachev, wife of the Soviet leader. On her visit to London in 1984 she went shopping for jewellery with a credit card. And in Paris she visited the showrooms of Pierre Cardin.

Average monthly wages in the 1980s:

	Roubles
Elite Party and state officials:	500 to 2,000
Coal miners:	298
Skilled manual workers:	230
All employees:	177
Doctors in polyclinics:	150
Primary school teachers:	rise slowly to 140
Librarians:	112
Minimum wage:	80

This may help to explain why such occupations receive lower pay than many manual jobs. But members of the intelligentsia often have the following advantages:
- better pensions and state benefits,
- access to extra income through private work,
- access to larger flats,
- access to better education (in 1982 the Soviet newspaper *Pravda* stated that the children of the intelligentsia are almost three times as likely as blue collar offspring to enter the professional ranks).

Social stratification

3 Routine white-collar workers

'Sluzhashchie' is the word used to distinguish unqualified or junior non-manual employees. Lane has divided this group into

(a) non-manual employees in
culture (for example, librarians),
local government (for example, clerks),
politics (for example, trade union officials);

(b) engineering-technical workers, that is, production workers with specialist qualifications (Lane regards these as 'non-manual members of the working class').

4 Blue-collar industrial workers

In 1919 the wages of the highest grades of workers were fixed at only 1.75 times those of the lowest paid. In 1921, when Lenin introduced the New Economic Policy, a wage structure was established with 17 divisions to cover all grades of employees. Highly skilled workers were given greater incentives with their wages at 3.5 times the wages of the lowest category and the ratio of the highest to the lowest salary was 8 to 1. Wage differentials were further widened under Stalin. As well as high wages, miners also have longer holidays, better access to health resorts and the right to retire five years earlier than other workers.

5 Agricultural workers

These work in two different sorts of enterprise:

State farms

Organised like a state-owned factory with a ministry-appointed director.

Employees seen as 'workers' with the same rights to state welfare services as those in other industries.

Collective farms

Co-operative production by peasant smallholders on land leased 'in perpetuity' to the collective.

Income depends on produce which is farmed and marketed co-operatively. Social security used to come from the farm's own funds, not the state.

Other dimensions of social stratification in the USSR

Rural dwellers

They comprise 37 per cent of the total population. They are generally thinly spread and have inferior welfare facilities, such as health and educational services.

Women

They tend to be in less skilled and lower paid work. As in the UK, on average they earn 66 per cent of male earnings.

Ethnic minorities

Participation in higher education is highest among Jews in the USSR and lowest in the Muslim Central Asian Republics.

For further reading see:
The Waking Giant: the Soviet Union under Gorbachev by Martin Walker (1986)
The End of Social Inequality? by David Lane (1982)
Soviet Economy and Society by David Lane (1985)
Modern Soviet Society by Basile Kerblay (1983)

Data-response questions

1 How did Peter the Great modernise the class system of feudal Russia?
2 How have wage differentials differed since the 1917 Revolution?
3 Members of the intelligentsia may have lower wages than certain skilled manual occupations but they often have a number of perks and privileges. List some of these advantages.
4 In what ways does the stratification system in the USSR differ from stratification in Britain? (See also p. 45).

Discussion

'There is no ruling class in the USSR because

- there is no property-owning wealthy class with great economic power,
- there is no closed elite passing political power from one generation to the next.'

Research suggestion

Hypothesis: Members of the working class have a different view of the social usefulness of jobs (such as nurses and stockbrokers) from members of the middle class.
Method: Select samples of middle- and working-class respondents and ask them to rank a list of a broad range of twenty occupations (from professional to unskilled) according to the social status which they think each job deserves.

9 Religion

Religion and social control

Source A: The social functions of religion

The term social control refers to aspects of society that produce unity and order. Many sociologists claim that religion is an important source of social control. It performs this function in a number of ways:

- All religions provide shared values and standards of behaviour. Without a general acceptance of some values between individuals a common way of life would be impossible and society would collapse. An example of a shared value is the Old Testament's Eighth Commandment, 'Thou shalt not steal'.
- Religion gives further support (sanction) to the rules and laws of society. Thus individuals are fearful of breaking certain rules because they may be punished by God as well as society.
- All religions have rituals and ceremonies which bring believers together and by doing so strengthen their commitment to a common way of life.

Source B: A Muslim girl talks about her faith

Naela is an 'A' Level student at Walthamstow School for Girls:

'Islam is a complete way of life. It must be appreciated then that the few remarks that I have recorded here only give the barest glimpse of that way of life.

I personally believe that Islam, after emphasising the greater importance of God, is based on human decency. As a Muslim I have been brought up to hold certain beliefs and to carry out certain practices which have shaped my life. I have to pray five times a day: at dawn, midday, before sunset, sunset and at nightfall. Islam states that Muslims should cover all parts of their bodies, with only hands, feet and face revealed. This particularly applies to women since it is believed that a woman's beauty should be hidden so as not to entice men.

Muslims are not allowed to hold a steady relationship with members of the opposite sex until marriage. Marriage should only take place with the permission of parents. Muslims are expected to show a great deal of respect towards other human beings, especially elders. As a result great importance is attached to hospitality. Muslims should treat even enemies as guests when they are in their homes.

My faith helps me to feel sensitive towards others. I feel that in caring for and loving others, I am caring for and loving myself and God. Muslims believe that everyday one should engage in at least one act of charity.

I believe most strongly that there is One God, *Allah*. Every incident favourable or unfavourable in my life, has strengthened my belief in *Allah* and the Islam faith. In every action that I perform, I am tested by *Allah* but without faith in *Allah* my life would be meaningless.'

Naela

Religion

Source C: A student talks about her atheism

Jacqui is an undergraduate student studying maths at University College, London:

'I think that the strongest influence on my beliefs has come from my two elder sisters. They are both atheists and believe that life is about living now. When you have no belief in God or an after-life it makes you live life to the full. I know some religious people who content themselves with living half a life now because they think that there is an after-life to come. I think that we would all benefit if there was no religion because then people might be more inclined to make this world a better place to live in.

Not believing in God is a belief in itself. I believe that the miracle of life is that it exists at all. It is fantastic that evolution has ended up with all this natural beauty, and human beings too. I'm lucky that I have life – and I intend to enjoy it. I believe that people are basically good and that if we treat each other in a decent way that goodness will shine through. My overriding purpose in life is to ensure that the people I care about and myself are happy. Also, I'm a socialist because I believe that everyone should have the opportunity to lead a happy and fulfilled life.

The biggest problem for atheists is posed by death. It is my belief that when you die you cease to be and your molecular structure ends up again in the nitrogen cycle. I read a book about Epicurus, a Greek philosopher, who was an atheist and believed in enjoying life now. His followers all had on their tombstones, "I was not, I have been, I am not, I don't mind". I used to think that that is what I would feel about death. But until someone you love dies you can never understand the ferocity of grief as an emotion. You "mind" very much. The question of death is something that I am still working on.'

Jacqui

Data-response questions

1 Using Source A, how is social control defined?
2 List three other agencies of social control apart from religion.
3 Using Source B:
   (a) List the ways in which Islam has affected Naela's relations with other people.
   (b) Give one example of how Islam acts as a form of social control for its followers.
   (c) According to Naela what is Islam based on?
4 Using Source C:
   (a) What is Jacqui's overriding purpose in life?
   (b) Jacqui's sisters have influenced her into accepting a certain attitude to life. Describe this attitude.
   (c) What do Naela and Jacqui have in common regarding their attitude towards other people? Use what they have written to support your answer.
5 What are the strengths and weaknesses of using sources such as B and C as sociological evidence?

Discussion

1 'Without religion there would be more social conflict.'
2 'All societies have some form of religion.'

Research suggestion

Hypothesis: Atheists are no less thoughtful of and caring towards others than religiously-minded people.
Method: Conduct in-depth interviews with a few religious and non-religious people.

Secularisation

Source A: Why sociologists disagree

Secularisation is the name sociologists give to the general loss of interest in religion. But the problem with measuring secularisation and deciding how far it has gone is defining religion in the first place. Though sociologists are broadly agreed that religion is in decline, they don't agree as to what religion actually *is*. As a result, there are several different approaches to the idea of secularisation:

Decline in churchgoing

Smaller congregations imply that there is less interest in religion, but they don't actually *prove* we are less religious. In the last century, churchgoing was a convention expected by society – it wasn't necessarily any proof of deep religious conviction.

Religion and the state

In England in the middle ages, the government and the church were almost inseparable. The king was literally 'defender of the faith', and the law of the land was God's law. Shakespeare's history plays provide a vivid picture of how bishops were as powerful as barons.

Things are very different today. Bishops still have their place in the House of Lords, but their voice is little heeded in public debate. Even fifty years ago, the church had a major say in the abdication crisis; recently, there have been occasions when the prime minister has been 'too busy' to see the Archbishop of Canterbury. As Bryan Wilson says: 'To invoke God in political dispute would today be regarded as, at best, bad taste.'

The broader view of religion

But could it be that sociologists have been taking too narrow a view of what religion is? One of the broadest modern definitions is by Peter Berger and Thomas Luckmann, who see religion simply as the display of identity, meaning and purpose in people's lives.

Luckmann has suggested that what we are experiencing is not necessarily *less* religion, but a shift from a narrow religion, which takes place in churches, to a wider, private one: many non-churchgoers may hold beliefs and take part in activities which may be loosely called 'religious'.

(adapted from 'Society Today' in *New Society*, 17 March 1983)

Source B

Can you enjoy your Christmas knowing what his will be like?

This picture was taken in the North of England.
It was not specially set up or reconstructed.
We just asked a photographer to record what he found in the cities of our country.
Peter is two years old.
He's just one of almost two million children living in appalling deprivation in Britain today.
Living in conditions that create family tensions, domestic violence and worse.
Christmas Day won't be very much different.
Every year The Children's Society helps thousands of such children.
For every child we help, however, there are many we can't.
This Christmas you could help us to help even more children next year.
Please send your donation to: Church of England Children's Society, Freepost, London WC1X 0BR.

Name
Address
Amount £
We're grateful for your donation, but to save us money we will not send a receipt unless you tick this box.
Access Barclaycard

The Children's Society. Needed now more than ever.

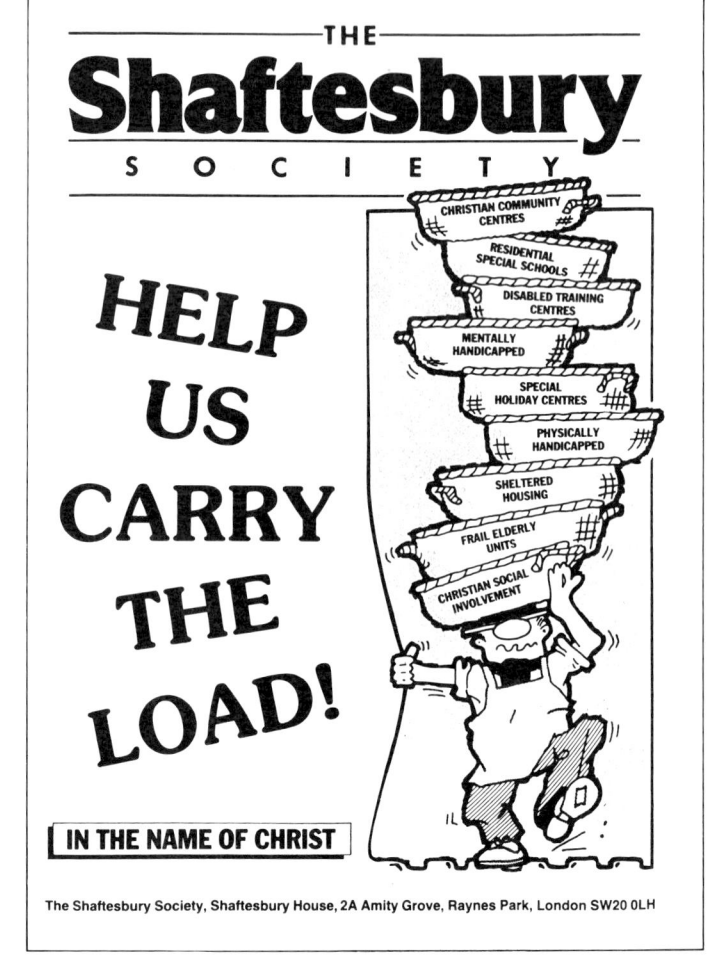

THE Shaftesbury SOCIETY

HELP US CARRY THE LOAD!

CHRISTIAN COMMUNITY CENTRES
RESIDENTIAL SPECIAL SCHOOLS
DISABLED TRAINING CENTRES
MENTALLY HANDICAPPED
SPECIAL HOLIDAY CENTRES
PHYSICALLY HANDICAPPED
SHELTERED HOUSING
FRAIL ELDERLY UNITS
CHRISTIAN SOCIAL INVOLVEMENT

IN THE NAME OF CHRIST

The Shaftesbury Society, Shaftesbury House, 2A Amity Grove, Raynes Park, London SW20 0LH

(from *21st Century Christian* magazine, December 1987)

Religion

Source C: How widespread are religious experiences?

So how religious are the British? We mean something deeper than whether people attend services, believe in religious creeds or obey their commandments. What interests us is something less tangible – the inner life that most of us rarely share with others.

In 1986 we placed a set of questions in a Gallup survey. The answers show that nearly half of the adult population of Britain believe they have had a religious or transcendental experience:

Table 1: National frequency of report of different types of experience

	percentage
Patterning of events	29
Awareness of the presence of God	27
Awareness of receiving help in answer to prayer	25
Awareness of a guiding presence not called God	22
Awareness of the presence of the dead	18
Awareness of a sacred presence in nature	16
Awareness of an evil presence	12
Experiencing that all things are one	5
Cumulative positive response rate	48

Table 2: Those interpreting their experiences religiously

	percentage
Awareness of the presence of God	80
Awareness of receiving help in answer to prayer	79
Awareness of a sacred presence in nature	61
Awareness of kindly presence looking after/guiding	58
Experiencing that all things are one	55
Awareness of an evil presence	38
Awareness of the presence of someone who has died	35
Patterning of events	32

(adapted from 'Religion is Good for You' by D. Hay and G. Heald in *New Society*, 17 April 1987)

Data-response questions

1 Using Source A:
   (a) What does secularisation mean?
   (b) Does the fall in churchgoing prove that we are less religious now?
   (c) Why does Luckmann believe that we are *not* less religious now?
2 Using Source B, how can you tell that both charities are Christian-based?
3 Using Source C:
   (a) What percentage of respondents had felt the presence of God?
   (b) Of those who had felt the presence of God, what proportion did *not* interpret this experience in a religious way?
4 Describe three types of evidence which could usefully contribute to the debate about secularisation.

Discussion

1 'A truly religious person would regularly attend a place of public worship.'
2 'The development of science has made religious beliefs less convincing.'

Research suggestion

Hypothesis: Although institutional religion may have declined, there is still a widespread belief that supernatural forces affect our lives.
Methods: 1 Give a questionnaire to a cross-section of people, with questions such as 'Have you had any supernatural experiences?' 2 Find out from newsagents, booksellers and librarians whether there is a great demand for books and magazines about religion and the supernatural.

Religious cults

Source A: The People's Temple

Jim Jones, born in 1931, began his religious career as a pastor at a Methodist church. After a disagreement, he left to set up his own religious organisation – the People's Temple. To raise funds for a church building, Jones went from door to door selling South American spider monkeys.

Jones had a strong desire to help the poor and he set up a soup kitchen for tramps and two nursing homes for the elderly and the sick. At the same time his ideas were becoming more strange. By 1950 he began to believe in reincarnation and that he was God's heir on earth. At about this time he also rejected the Bible as an insult to God.

An increasing number of people attended his church lured by the attraction of witnessing 'miracle healings'. Needless to say, all of these were fakes. It is estimated that the membership of the People's Temple was at one time as high as 1.4 million. Jones successfully created the impression that his church was a respectable religious organisation and that he was a responsible religious leader. As a consequence, he mixed with national politicians and even had dinner with Rosalyn Carter, President Carter's wife. Jones was appointed by the Mayor of Indianapolis to be the first full-time director of a human rights commission.

Meanwhile, the church's members were treated as slaves. They were kept in a state of physical exhaustion, poverty and fear. Jones regularly told his followers to drink a liquid which he said would kill them after 45 minutes. When the 45 minutes had passed, Jones informed them that drinking the liquid was an exercise to test their loyalty to the cause. He called this test the 'white night ritual'. Jones often demanded sexual favours from his followers – both men and women. Once an individual had joined the church it was very difficult to leave; some who did leave died in mysterious circumstances afterwards.

In 1977 Jones told his followers that they were about to suffer persecution and that they should flee with him to the Amazon jungle where he had bought some land.

Many unpleasant stories began to circulate about the People's Temple and a United States Congressman, Leo Ryan, decided to investigate. Jones invited him to the Temple's hideout in the Amazon. Ryan, some journalists and relatives set off in a plane on 17 November 1978. They had a very welcoming reception and all seemed to be well. The trouble started when a grandmother pleaded with Ryan to get her out and then a number of other members made the same desperate request. Ryan was nearly stabbed by one of Jones's followers but he and his group escaped towards their aircraft. Unfortunately, before they managed to take off seven of them were shot dead, three journalists, three escaping followers and Ryan.

At 5 pm on 18 November 1978, Jones called all his followers together and told them that the plane would be shot down but that eventually the camp would be invaded and destroyed. Jones shouted 'If we cannot live in peace, then let us die in peace.' He continued, 'Take the poison like they used to in ancient Greece.' A very large container was brought forward. It consisted of a liquid mixed in with which was cyanide. Everyone took a drink and 913 members of the People's Temple including Jones and 260 children died.

Jim Jones was once a respected social leader, with carefully developed political connections. By the end he was a paranoid dictator, surviving on alternate stimulants and tranquillizers.

Jones's empty throne overlooks the carnage of the 'white night'. Beneath the throne, a voice-activated tape-recorder took down all that happened on that appalling night.

Source B: Why do people join the Moonie cult?

Those who joined as full-time members living in Unification Church centres tended to be:

- idealistic and young, aged eighteen to twenty-eight;
- middle-class achievers from secure, sheltered families;
- males without a steady and satisfying relationship with a girlfriend;
- people with a strong sense of service, duty and responsibility;
- people with a desire to help improve the world;
- people for whom religious questions are important.

(adapted from *The Making of a Moonie: Choice or Brainwashing?* by Eileen Barker, Basil Blackwell 1984)

Source C: Denomination, sect or cult?

Why are some religious organisations called churches while others are best described as denominations, sects or cults? The sort of definitions that sociologists might use are as follows:

A church is a stable organisation of religious believers with a fixed body of doctrine which ties in with the accepted beliefs of society. In Britain, the most obvious example is the Church of England which has the Queen as its head.

A denomination is one of a number of minority religious organisations that are broadly considered acceptable by society. Protestant denominations in Britain include the Methodists and the United Reformed Church.

A sect is smaller and less formally organised than a church or denomination. It is often inward-looking and sometimes at odds with the beliefs of society as a whole. Sects are usually formed by people protesting about established religion straying from the 'correct' teaching and they are often very strict in outlook, such as the Jehovah's Witnesses.

Cults are similar to sects, but they are more concerned with finding new ways to salvation rather than returning to old ones. They are often based around the discovery of a new 'prophet', such as the Rev. Sun Myung Moon of the 'Moonies' or the Rev. Jim Jones of the People's Temple.

(adapted from *New Society*, 17 March 1983)

Data-response questions

1. Using Source A:
   (a) How did Jim Jones test the loyalty of his followers?
   (b) Describe the events that led to the mass suicide.
   (c) How did Jim Jones manage to achieve the control that he had over his followers?
2. From Source B, name some categories of people who would *not* be typical full-time Moonies?
3. Using Source C:
   (a) Give an example of a denomination.
   (b) In which category would you place the People's Temple?
   (c) Give two characteristics of churches and two characteristics of sects.
4. Discuss the difficulties for a sociologist wishing to study a religious cult.

Discussion

'No human being deserves to be worshipped. Hero worship is dangerous both for the hero or heroine and the followers.'

Research suggestion

Hypothesis: Cults are always created by individuals with powerful personalities. Most cease to exist after a short period of time but some turn into sects and then into established churches (e.g. the Mormons).

Method: Use the historical, sociological and religious sections of your local library to find studies of cults. Provide a brief outline of the emergence, beliefs and development of a number of cults. (Primary research into cults is not recommended. It could involve risks for the researcher!)

10 The media

Violence and the media

Source **A**

as MPs call for crackdown on video violence

mac

AFTERMATH OF THE MASSACRE

Outrage over film nasties after the Rambo killings

Low-budget movie that started the sick trend

By SHAUN USHER

THREE years before Clint Eastwood's Dirty Harry, a low-budget Hollywood movie was doing the rounds.

It made the reputation of its almost unknown director, Peter Bogdanovich, started a trend and coined the phrase 'random killer movie.'

It was called Targets, and told the story of a psychopathic sniper who picked off victims at random in a drive-in movie theatre.

Hollywood took notice. Three years later Clint Eastwood's Dirty Harry took up the gun that Targets had introduced.

It was violent. Far more violent.

One of Dirty Harry's first scenes showed a half-naked girl being shot dead in a swimming pool. The murderer was a random killer, using a high-powered rifle.

Ever since, there has been an unrelenting succession of random killer movies, in the cinemas and on our television screens.

Each film has striven to find new ways to saturate the screen with more blood than the last, seeking new and more gruesome ways to lavish it there.

Here is a list of just a few of the more memorable ones:

Eastwood in Dirty Harry

Magnum Force: Random killers terrorise San Francisco, hunted by Clint Eastwood.
Two Minute Warning: Random killer at football stadium.
Death Wish: Vigilante turns random killer of muggers.

Violent

Taxi Driver: Random killer, a Viet vet, runs amok in New York.
Invasion USA: Random killer shoots 200 Russians.
Cobra: Cop after random killers murders 36 himself.
Armed Response: Random killer murders ten Chinese.
Terminator: Futuristic random killer-cop murders dozens as he hunts his prey.
Helter Skelter: Charles Manson's random killings.
Friday The 13th: Teenage campers slaughtered on their wooded site by a random killer. Betsy Palmer responsible for the deaths.
Friday The 13th – Part 2: More teenagers find their campsite becomes a slaughterhouse from the random killer.
The Sniper: A mentally-deranged man who can't prevent himself being the random killer of women.
In Cold Blood: Two youngsters who believe themselves to be above the law are the random killers of a complete family.
Halloween: Random killer slaughters helpless teenagers.
Nightmare On Elm Street: Random killer haunts four teenagers to the grave.
If: Horror at public school as random killers machine gun hundreds at school.
Boston Strangler: Tony Curtis is the random killer whose rise, manhunt and capture is based on reality.
The Texas Chainsaw Massacre: Random killing family who find their victims among the travellers in Texas.
Rambo: Crazed Viet-veteran turns random killer to escape his hunters.

By GORDON GREIG

LEADING MPs are calling for a new crackdown on TV and video violence after the Rambo-style Hungerford massacre.

They are acutely worried by the slide towards sickening scenes of horror in videos freely available in High Street shops.

Two years ago the Daily Mail led a campaign to clean up video nasties. It resulted in the Government establishing a new licensing system on who could rent or buy pornographic videos.

Former Tory Minister Dr Rhodes Boyson said last night: 'It's time we had a new Bill or tighter rules on what is becoming a frightening situation in the display of blood and death on TV and the video market.

'This sort of violence degrades all human life. And at some point we are going to see people walk out of the artificial life they've been watching on TV and into the real one on the streets and play the same part.

Attacked

Mr Ivor Stanbrook attacked the import of violent films from the U.S.

Mr Stanbrook, Tory MP for Orpington and a member of the Commons Select Committee on Home Affairs, said: 'Films of the Rambo type undoubtedly affect weak or diseased minds.'

The Tory Home Affairs Committee is to discuss pushing through a Private Members Bill to tighten up on the new generation of violent videos if the Government is reluctant to act.

Meanwhile in Hungerford itself, video shop trader Roger Sandford yesterday removed all copies of the Rambo and Commando films

Suicide ends hunt for triple killer

A MAN who killed his wife and two children was found dead in a river yesterday.

Ivor 'Rod' Shirley is thought to have planned the murders and suicide at least a week ago when he made a will which benefits two conservationist societies.

Mr Shirley, 44, was recently sacked from his engineering job with tractor makers Massey Ferguson following investigations into the theft of parts worth thousands of pounds from the company.

The triple murder at the family's home in Hampton Magna, Warwickshire, was discovered by solicitor John Hathaway who drew up Mr Shirley's will.

In it, Mr Shirley left his estate to his wife. In the event of her death it would go to the children and in the event of their deaths to two charities.

'On Wednesday we received a letter from Mr Shirley, which, from its tone, suggested that something may be amiss at the family home.' said Mr Hathaway yesterday.

Battered

Shortly afterwards the solicitor received a phone call from the chairman of the British Butterfly Conservation Society of Quorn in Leicestershire, who had received a letter from Mr Shirley saying: 'You will have read in the Press of my death and the deaths of the members of my family and I wish to inform you that you are principal beneficiaries under my will.'

Mr Hathaway went to the Shirleys' home, looked through a gap in the curtains – and called the police.

Inside were the battered bodies of Mrs Diane Shirley, 43, her 20-year-old son Paul and daughter Katheryn, aged 17.

Later Mr Hathaway discovered that a letter similar to that received by the butterfly charity had been sent to the Warwickshire Nature Conservation Trust.

(from the *Daily Mail*, 21 August 1987)

Source B: Research into the effects of violence on television

The Independent Broadcasting Authority's latest research indicates that 6 per cent of viewers sometimes feel violent after watching violent television programmes. Three thousand viewers were asked whether they agreed with the statement: 'Sometimes I feel quite violent after watching crime programmes.'

But Dr Guy Cumberbatch, who has studied television violence for the BBC, believes that this research is flawed. 'It was a silly question,' he said. . . .

The IBA team should, according to Cumberbatch, have followed up the question they did ask with additional questions designed to uncover whether people had actually become violent after watching programmes and whether they had felt violent before watching certain programmes.

The research also failed to identify the people who had violent feelings. 'Were they senior citizens, or juvenile delinquents?' Cumberbatch asked, adding that the IBA research was 'disappointing'.

Cumberbatch says that when viewers are asked if there is too much violence on television, they will agree. But when more in-depth research is carried out, the conclusions are different.

In a follow-up study for the BBC, Cumberbatch is exploring whether there is a connection between violent programmes and the audience ratings figures they achieve. This study, which will be completed in two months' time, is already turning up fascinating results. Cumberbatch says: 'It looks as if violent programmes do attract larger audiences.' This finding appears to contradict opinion polls and the IBA research, where viewers say they are worried about violence on television.

This will present broadcasters and the government with a problem. British broadcasters are engaged in a massive effort to lower the amount of violence on television. At the same time, the established broadcasters face the prospect of real competition. Later this year, the launch of the first of a flock of satellites is planned. Many channels are likely to originate outside the UK and will therefore not be subject to the tough standards demanded by the government.

So, if it is true that to get high ratings broadcasters must continue to give viewers the violent programmes they seem to want, they are bound to lose audiences.

(from *The Sunday Times*, 31 January 1988)

Q Data-response questions

1. Using Source A:
   (a) What type of film does the phrase 'random killer movies' refer to?
   (b) Why is Dr Rhodes Boyson worried about video violence?
2. Using Source B:
   (a) What conclusion did the IBA research reach regarding audience reaction to television violence?
   (b) What question did the IBA researchers ask viewers?
   (c) Why does Dr Cumberbatch think that the IBA's research is seriously flawed.
   (d) The IBA reported that 60 per cent of viewers felt that there was too much violence on television. How does Dr Cumberbatch's research cast doubt on this finding?
   (e) The IBA and the BBC have decided to reduce the amount of violence in their programmes. What problem might this decision cause them?
3. Why is it difficult, if not impossible, to prove the effects of television violence on viewers' behaviour?

D Discussion

1. What do we mean by violence and violent programmes on television?
2. 'Watching screen violence is, on balance, good for us since it helps to get rid of our violent emotions in a harmless way.'

R Research suggestion

Hypothesis: While people feel that there is too much violence on television they actually enjoy watching violent programmes.

Method: Prepare a questionnaire investigating people's views about TV violence and which programmes they watch regularly. The questionnaire could be given to an equal number of people in different age groups. This would enable you to make comparisons between the responses of the different age groups.

Political bias in the press

Source A

Daily Express
WEDNESDAY MARCH 16 1988

Lawson's historic tax revolution sparks an unprecedented row in the Commons

WE'RE ALL IN THE MONEY!

Nigel gives families extra £6 each week

TAXES started tumbling last night as Chancellor Nigel Lawson crowned the Thatcher revolution with the most historic and radical Budget since the war.

Source B

Daily Mirror
Wednesday, March 16, 1988   FORWARD WITH BRITAIN   20p

BUDGET '88

ALL OR NOTHING

It's tax cuts galore, but NOT if you're poor

By JULIA LANGDON, Political Editor

CHANCELLOR Nigel Lawson yesterday produced a Budget to help the rich get richer — and left the rest with the small change.

He lashed out £4,000 million... and nearly everything went to those who needed it least.

Source C

MIRROR COMMENT

Soaking the poor

DESPAIR, desperation and destitution began yesterday for millions of decent men and women — and their children.

To make it worse, many didn't know the full extent of what was happening. Or why. Or who was responsible.

They said so in calls to the Daily Mirror. In anguished visits to overburdened DHSS offices. In inquiries to advice bureaux, charities and MPs.

Not since the means tests of the 1930s, which forced unemployed families to sell all but a few sticks of furniture before they could get any benefit, has a British Government taken away so much from those who have so little.

Not since then has there been so much confusion, heartbreak and real fear. Not without cause. The reduced social security benefits lock up the chronically sick and disabled tighter and deeper in a prison of poverty.

Survive

AND deserted wives and abandoned single parents. AND pensioners who have spent a lifetime saving for their old age and a proper funeral.

AND *the unemployed.* AND *those trying to survive on subsistence wages.*

Those in need aren't to be helped — or heard. They are to be swept under the Persian carpet at No 10.

What will the Tories do next? Open privatised soup kitchens?

(from the *Daily Mirror*, 12 April 1988)

Source D

THE SUN SAYS
Santa kicks the bucket

UNTIL today, the Welfare State had not been overhauled for more than 40 years.

The system was chaotic. Many people did not even know which benefit they could claim.

Social Security devours £50billion a year—a tenth of the national income.

Despite bleating from the Socialists, that bill has been increased by a further £300million a year.

In future benefits will be more directly related to need.

There will be losers.

Some low earners will no longer be encouraged not to work because they can get more on the dole.

Principle

Unemployed youngsters will be tempted to leave home to find jobs.

Thrifty old people who have savings will suffer.

Yet if they have money they need less help.

The Sun believes there is a precious principle that no one should go hungry or live in deprivation through no fault of his or her own.

Yet it is **ALSO** a precious principle that people must learn to fend for themselves whenever they can do so.

Their first reaction should be to decide what they can do for themselves rather than what the State can do for them.

Sad as it may be there is no such thing as Santa Claus. The nation has to look after itself.

(from the *Sun*, 11 April 1988)

Data-response questions

1 With reference to Sources A and B:
   (a) Which newspaper did not support the Conservative government's 1988 budget?
   (b) How much did the Chancellor of the Exchequer 'give away' in tax cuts?
   (c) Income tax was cut from 60 per cent to 40 per cent at the higher rate and from 27 per cent to 25 per cent at the basic rate (a saving of £6 per week to a family of four earning £16,000 a year) while taxes on beer and cigarettes were increased. How would these changes affect someone living on welfare benefits?
   (d) Which of the two newspapers offers the most accurate summary of the budget in its headline?
2 Using Sources C and D, how did the editorials of the *Sun* and the *Daily Mirror* differ in their opinions of the changes made to the social security system in April 1988?
3 Describe three methods newspapers use to influence their readers.
4 Why are sociologists interested in examining newspapers?

Discussion

'While the newspapers are openly politically biased, the television stations are carefully balanced and impartial in their political coverage.'

Research suggestion

Hypothesis: People choose newspapers which reinforce rather than change their political prejudices.

Method: Interview readers of newspapers which openly support the Conservative or Labour parties. Ask them
- how long they have been reading the newspaper,
- whether their own opinions have altered since taking the paper,
- whether they think the paper has influenced their political views,
- which political party they support.

Elections and the media

Source A: The decline of local political party organisation in general election campaigns

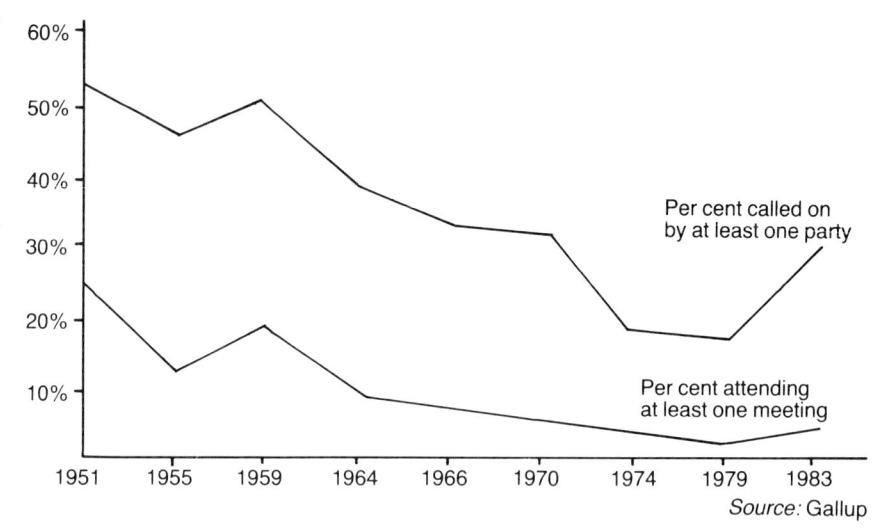

[Graph showing two declining lines from 1951 to 1983. Upper line labelled "Per cent called on by at least one party" starts around 53% in 1951 and ends around 30% in 1983. Lower line labelled "Per cent attending at least one meeting" starts around 25% in 1951 and ends around 5% in 1983. X-axis years: 1951, 1955, 1959, 1964, 1966, 1970, 1974, 1979, 1983.]

Source: Gallup

(from 'Voters' by M. Harrop in *The Media in British Politics* edited by J. Seaton and B. Pimlott, Gower, 1987)

Source B: A campaign of 'stupefying frightfulness'

Although television is obliged to present 'balanced' political coverage, newspapers are free to take a partisan line. During general elections the press might be expected to become even more partisan than usual, but in May and June 1987 the behaviour of certain newspapers was seen by some people as reaching new depths of bias, lies and distortion.

Early in the election campaign, the *Sun* and the *Star* published 'lies, smears and scandals' about David Steel's personal life. David Steel successfully sued the papers and spoke with contempt of 'the gutter press who are debasing this whole election'. It was rumoured that a team of 'journalists' from one national newspaper had even questioned Neil Kinnock's neighbours in their attempt to manufacture scandals and complaints. Mr Kinnock said on 26 May: 'We now have a press which in sections is more irresponsible, more prone to slander, more filthy than we have had in this country before.'

The *Sun* carried 'interviews', via a medium and psychic investigator, with figures such as Stalin, Henry the VIII and Lord Nelson. Boadicea, who died over 1900 years ago, stated in the *Sun*: 'When I hear the words of Kinnock and his treacherous ilk I feel ashamed for England.' The *Sun* ran a campaign in favour of the Conservatives of 'Stupefying frightfulness', according to Hugh Stephenson in the *Guardian*. On 10 June the *Sun* urged their readers not to let 'Kinnock's crackpots wreck Maggie's revolution'.

(adapted from 'General Election 1987' by John Benyon in *Social Studies Review*, November 1987)

Source C

	Readers' assessment of their newspapers' party support				The party support of the newspapers' readers			
	Con %	Lab %	Lib/SDP %	None/Don't Know %	Con %	Lab %	Lib/SDP %	Other %
Conservative papers[a]								
Daily Express	87	0	4	9	70	9	18	3
The Daily Telegraph	85	0	3	12	80	5	10	5
Sunday Express	80	2	4	14	64	6	25	5
Daily Mail	78	2	5	15	60	13	19	8
The Sunday Telegraph	78	2	2	18	78	9	9	4
The Sunday Times	69	5	13	13	58	15	23	4
The Mail on Sunday	68	5	8	19	61	14	20	5
The Sun	63	12	7	18	41	31	19	9
The Times	61	0	33	6	56	12	27	5
News of the World	42	15	5	38	37	33	23	7
The Star	23	16	7	54	28	46	18	8
Labour papers[a]								
Daily Mirror	2	84	8	6	20	55	21	4
Sunday Mirror	5	73	5	17	25	49	19	7
The People	10	41	6	43	36	38	20	6
The Guardian	13	30	43	14	22	54	19	5
Alliance paper[a]								
Today	11	4	18	67	43	17	40	0
Non-partisan papers[a]								
The Independent	12	6	20	62	34	34	27	5
The Observer	13	35	31	21	28	49	18	5

Source: MORI poll during the 1987 general election campaign.
Note: (a) The partisanship of each newspaper is derived from its voting recommendation for the 1987 general election;
(b) Figures are not available for the *Financial Times* (which supported the Conservative Party).

(from 'General Election 1987')

Source D: The electoral impact of the partisan press

The data in Source C suggests that the influence of newspapers on their readers' voting behaviour is not as great as some people might imagine. It has been argued that in general the mass media confirm rather than change existing opinions, although if the reader doesn't have views on a subject newspapers may help to establish them.

However, the political influence of the press during elections is more subtle than just converting their readers to their party colours. Election campaigns are largely conducted on television, which has become a principal source of political information. But how is the agenda set for television? Who decides the political issues and how they should be handled? It has long been argued that newspapers are significant in establishing the national news agenda which is adopted by broadcasters. The majority of people appear to make decisions about politics on the basis of images. Newspapers play an important part in creating and maintaining the predominant images about issues, politicians and parties, and thereby exercise influence over electoral behaviour.

So although the direct influence of newspapers on readers' voting behaviour may not be as strong as many believe, their electoral impact should not be underestimated. Both in setting the agenda and establishing the main issues, and also in creating the images of the parties and leading personalities, newspapers play a key role. The distortion and bias in the information provided by the overwhelmingly Conservative press to the public during an election campaign – and at other times – remains a significant feature of British politics.

(adapted from 'General Election 1987')

Data-response questions

1 Using Source A:
  (a) How has canvassing (doorstep campaigning) changed since 1951?
  (b) Why do people now rely more on the media for information during general elections than in the past?
2 Using Source B:
  (a) What does the word 'partisan' mean? Use a dictionary, if necessary.
  (b) Explain the meaning of David Steel's words, 'the gutter press who are debasing this whole election'.
  (c) What was the *Sun's* main aim in conducting 'interviews' with great figures from the past?
3 Using Source C:
  (a) What percentage of *Daily Express* readers vote for the Conservative party and see the *Daily Express* as a Conservative newspaper?
  (b) Why does the data suggest that the influence of newspapers on their reader's voting behaviour is fairly weak?
4 Using Source D:
  (a) Where in the main are elections now conducted?
  (b) Write a paragraph describing the 'indirect' influence of the press on elections.

Discussion

1 'The first responsibility of newspapers is not to entertain but to provide an accurate account of what goes on in the world.'
2 'Newspapers should not, as a general rule, pry into the private lives of politicians.'

Research suggestion

Hypothesis: At least two-thirds of the national press support the Conservative party.
Method: Look for political bias in the editorials of every paper on a particular day.

The ownership of the media

Source **A**

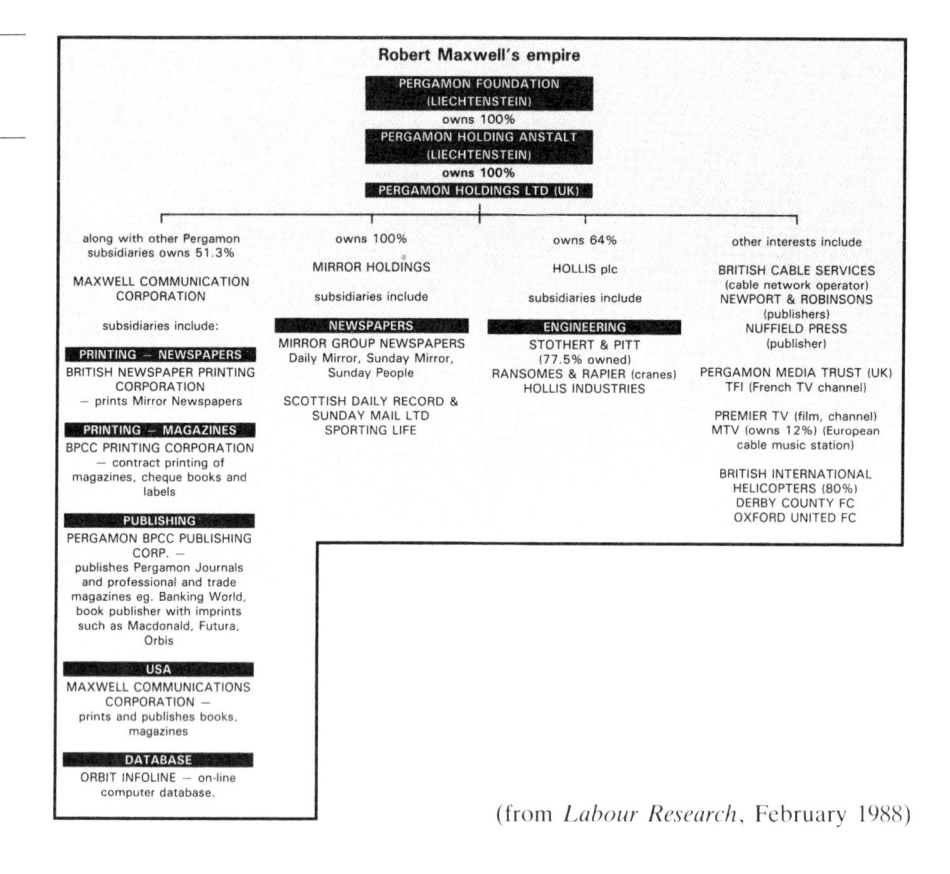

Robert Maxwell's empire

PERGAMON FOUNDATION (LIECHTENSTEIN)
owns 100%
PERGAMON HOLDING ANSTALT (LIECHTENSTEIN)
owns 100%
PERGAMON HOLDINGS LTD (UK)

along with other Pergamon subsidiaries owns 51.3%

MAXWELL COMMUNICATION CORPORATION

subsidiaries include:

PRINTING – NEWSPAPERS
BRITISH NEWSPAPER PRINTING CORPORATION
– prints Mirror Newspapers

PRINTING – MAGAZINES
BPCC PRINTING CORPORATION
– contract printing of magazines, cheque books and labels

PUBLISHING
PERGAMON BPCC PUBLISHING CORP. –
publishes Pergamon Journals and professional and trade magazines eg. Banking World, book publisher with imprints such as Macdonald, Futura, Orbis

USA
MAXWELL COMMUNICATIONS CORPORATION –
prints and publishes books, magazines

DATABASE
ORBIT INFOLINE — on-line computer database.

owns 100%

MIRROR HOLDINGS

subsidiaries include

NEWSPAPERS
MIRROR GROUP NEWSPAPERS
Daily Mirror, Sunday Mirror, Sunday People

SCOTTISH DAILY RECORD & SUNDAY MAIL LTD
SPORTING LIFE

owns 64%

HOLLIS plc

subsidiaries include

ENGINEERING
STOTHERT & PITT (77.5% owned)
RANSOMES & RAPIER (cranes)
HOLLIS INDUSTRIES

other interests include

BRITISH CABLE SERVICES (cable network operator)
NEWPORT & ROBINSONS (publishers)
NUFFIELD PRESS (publisher)

PERGAMON MEDIA TRUST (UK)
TF1 (French TV channel)

PREMIER TV (film, channel)
MTV (owns 12%) (European cable music station)

BRITISH INTERNATIONAL HELICOPTERS (80%)
DERBY COUNTY FC
OXFORD UNITED FC

(from *Labour Research*, February 1988)

Source **B**

The proud new owner

The media

Source C

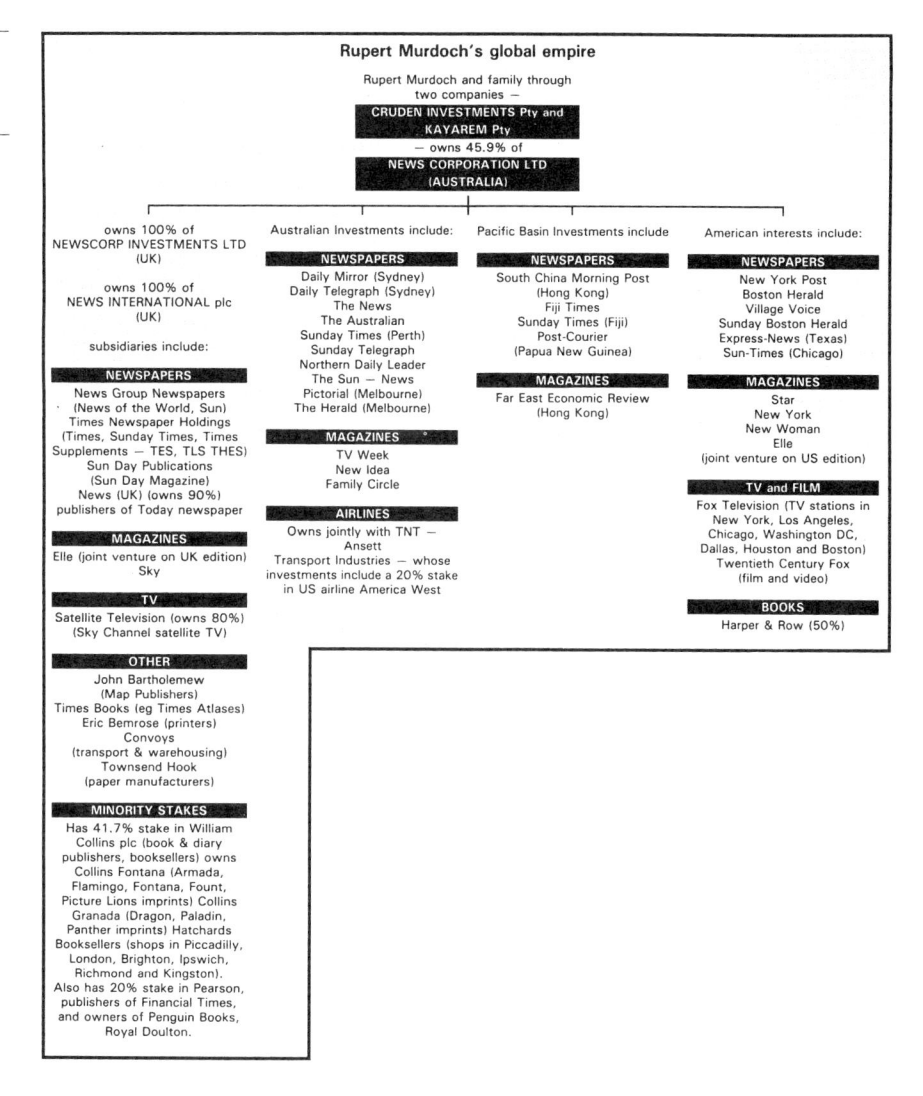

Rupert Murdoch's global empire

Rupert Murdoch and family through two companies —
CRUDEN INVESTMENTS Pty and KAYAREM Pty
— owns 45.9% of
NEWS CORPORATION LTD (AUSTRALIA)

owns 100% of NEWSCORP INVESTMENTS LTD (UK)

owns 100% of NEWS INTERNATIONAL plc (UK)

subsidiaries include:

NEWSPAPERS
News Group Newspapers
(News of the World, Sun)
Times Newspaper Holdings
(Times, Sunday Times, Times Supplements — TES, TLS THES)
Sun Day Publications
(Sun Day Magazine)
News (UK) (owns 90%)
publishers of Today newspaper

MAGAZINES
Elle (joint venture on UK edition)
Sky

TV
Satellite Television (owns 80%)
(Sky Channel satellite TV)

OTHER
John Bartholemew
(Map Publishers)
Times Books (eg Times Atlases)
Eric Bemrose (printers)
Convoys
(transport & warehousing)
Townsend Hook
(paper manufacturers)

MINORITY STAKES
Has 41.7% stake in William Collins plc (book & diary publishers, booksellers) owns Collins Fontana (Armada, Flamingo, Fontana, Fount, Picture Lions imprints) Collins Granada (Dragon, Paladin, Panther imprints) Hatchards Booksellers (shops in Piccadilly, London, Brighton, Ipswich, Richmond and Kingston).
Also has 20% stake in Pearson, publishers of Financial Times, and owners of Penguin Books, Royal Doulton.

Australian Investments include:

NEWSPAPERS
Daily Mirror (Sydney)
Daily Telegraph (Sydney)
The News
The Australian
Sunday Times (Perth)
Sunday Telegraph
Northern Daily Leader
The Sun — News
Pictorial (Melbourne)
The Herald (Melbourne)

MAGAZINES
TV Week
New Idea
Family Circle

AIRLINES
Owns jointly with TNT —
Ansett
Transport Industries — whose investments include a 20% stake in US airline America West

Pacific Basin Investments include

NEWSPAPERS
South China Morning Post (Hong Kong)
Fiji Times
Sunday Times (Fiji)
Post-Courier
(Papua New Guinea)

MAGAZINES
Far East Economic Review (Hong Kong)

American interests include:

NEWSPAPERS
New York Post
Boston Herald
Village Voice
Sunday Boston Herald
Express-News (Texas)
Sun-Times (Chicago)

MAGAZINES
Star
New York
New Woman
Elle
(joint venture on US edition)

TV and FILM
Fox Television (TV stations in New York, Los Angeles, Chicago, Washington DC, Dallas, Houston and Boston)
Twentieth Century Fox
(film and video)

BOOKS
Harper & Row (50%)

(from *Labour Research*, February 1988)

Q Data-response questions

1 Using Source B:
  (a) Why is Robert Maxwell looking so pleased?
  (b) How does the front page show the power of the proprietor?
2 Using Source A:
  (a) List the major newspaper titles owned by Robert Maxwell.
  (b) What other media interests are included in Robert Maxwell's 'empire'?
3 Using Source C:
  (a) To which continents of the world does Rupert Murdoch's 'global empire' extend?
  (b) Which newspaper titles does Rupert Murdoch own in Britain?

D Discussion

'In a healthy democracy the ownership of the media should not be concentrated into just a few hands.'

R Research suggestion

Compare the coverage of political events in the *Sun* with the coverage of political events in the *Daily Mirror*.

11 Politics

Pressure groups

Source **A**

Jane Smith (picture by Justin Leighton) combats experiments like those top right

Last Saturday's bomb in Selfridge's London store was the latest move by the Animal Liberation Front. Frances Rafferty, below, looks at both sides of the anti vivisection issue

Youth joins the fray

MORE AND MORE young people are becoming involved in the animal rights movement. But are all the issues as clear-cut as they seem?

Jane Smith, 24, of Charlton, South London presents an extreme view. Jane believes that animals and humans should have equal rights — even if it means halting development of a new drug.

She has been arrested during a demonstration and has raided laboratories.

She explained why she is prepared to break the law for her cause: " Direct action is the only way to publicise our cause. Animals are being tortured by big business — and the Government will do nothing."

Jane works at a cat sanctuary and is also a vegan — that is she doesn't eat meat, fish, eggs or dairy products or wear leather.

Jane had her first taste of action when she joined a demonstration at a Beecham's laboratory when her friend was arrested.

She said: "I don't believe humans have the right to say that we are the most important species. I can see no reason why we are. Animals can feel pain, just like us.

"I think factory farming is disgusting. If you come face to face with battery hens you can see how cruel it is.

"When we buy meat pre-packed from a supermarket, we don't think about it as an animal. We even call it a different name, for example beef. But it doesn't take much effort to be a vegetarian."

Jane outlined some animal liberationist action: "I took part in a daytime raid on an agricultural research lab which was looking into ways to fatten up animals for eating. We took photographs and information, but didn't damage anything."

She says she does not agree with the pharmaceutical industry testing their drugs on animals: " I personally wouldn't want to sacrifice an animal's life for my own. They have as much right to live as I do."

Putting the case forward for using animals for experiments in the drugs industry is David Parker of ICI. He explained: " ICI does carry out research involving animals. We are trying to combat serious diseases and are obliged by law, in the Medicines Act 1968, to carry out tests before using a drug or chemical on a human being.

" But it isn't just the legal aspect, it is also for moral reasons. We don't want any of our employees or the public to come in contact with a product that isn't safe.

" The animal rights people paint us all as sadists, but a lot of our scientsts own pets. They work with animals because there is no alternative."

ICI says their use of animals is declining and they have spent £8½ million looking into alternative techniques.

And Frances Charles-worth of the Animals in Medicine Research Information Centre (Amric) said: " When you are young it is difficult to think about illness and disease. Nobody wants to use animals, but if you want to test a new drug there is no choice. The bottom line is about saving people's lives."

(from the *Guardian*, 2 December 1987)

Source B

NHS patients' lobby keeps up pressure

ANNABEL FERRIMAN ■ Health Correspondent

HOSPITAL ALERT, the London-based patients' pressure group which embarrassed the Prime Minister by organising the highly-publicised doctors' petition to Downing Street in December, is widening its scope to become a national body next month.

It has already found co-ordinators in 68 constituencies for a mass lobby of Parliament on 25 February and has contacted every community health council in Britain.

Thousands of patients are expected to lobby their MPs and ask them to sign an early day motion, tabled last week, calling for the Chancellor, Nigel Lawson, to put an extra £2.5 billion into the health service in his Budget next month.

'The response has been overwhelming,' said the group's organiser, Julia Schofield of Twickenham. She hopes to link up with other voluntary groups nationwide to ensure continuing pressure on the Government. 'Patients have never had an effective voice in the NHS and we think it is time to put that right,' she said.

After protests by doctors and strikes by nurses, the lobby and the emergence of the new national group co-ordinating action by NHS consumers could gravely embarrass the Government.

Mrs Schofield's organisation, which she set up after waiting six months for a routine operation at the West Middlesex Hospital, achieved wide publicity in December when it organised a petition from 1,000 hospital consultants to the Prime Minister.

Mrs Schofield said: 'I have always been grateful to the NHS because it saved my life as a child. I was the first baby to be successfully operated on for a hiatus hernia. As I was the fifth child in a low-income family, we could never have paid for the operation.

Organiser: Schofield.

'Since then I have had nine operations on the NHS. If the health service were abolished, and we all had to rely on private insurance, I would be one of the many people who would be uninsurable because I am such a poor risk.'

(from the *Observer*, 7 February 1988)

Q Data-response questions

1. Using Source A:
   (a) What is the name of the pressure group referred to in this source?
   (b) What reason does Jane Smith give for using 'direct action'?
   (c) Give examples of direct action that Jane Smith has been involved in.
   (d) How would you describe the aim of this pressure group?
   (e) What evidence is given of the campaign's impact on the drugs industry?
2. Using Source B:
   (a) Give the name of the pressure group referred to in this source.
   (b) What is the aim of this pressure group?
   (c) Write a paragraph comparing the methods used by this pressure group with those used by the group discussed in Source A.
3. List the methods that a pressure group could use that are not mentioned in either Source A or Source B.

D Discussion

'In this society there are legal means available to us to influence public opinion. Therefore, there is no justification for a pressure group to break the law.'

R Research suggestion

Carry out a study of a pressure group. This study should include a description of the group's aims, methods, organisation and type of membership.

Gypsy site simulation

THE COUNTY TIMES

ADVERSALE GYPSY SITE ROW

Borsetshire Council's plan to provide the county's second permanent gypsy site just outside the small village of Adversale has quickly run into a storm of protest.

Mrs Palethorpe, proprietor of the Adversale Hotel, has called for an emergency meeting of Adversale's Parish Council. Local residents will then be able to express their views to representatives from the County Council. "It's bad enough having gypsies living on the lay-by just up the road," said Mrs Palethorpe "but a permanent site would absolutely ruin this pretty village."

PROPERTY VALUES

One aspect of the proposal which is causing local concern is the likely effect on house prices. Mr Henry Witty is a newcomer on the recent exclusive development by Detached Homes Ltd. He stated, "I came here to retire because it was quiet and unspoilt. The gypsy site will make many of us think about selling up and moving out. But will any one want to buy our homes?"

COUNCIL'S OBLIGATIONS

Ms Pam Macken, the County Planning Officer, pointed out that the Council still has to make the provision required by the 1968 Caravan Sites Act. A few permanent sites spread across the county would mean the end of caravans parked on the roadside. Six of the twenty pitches on the new site would be short-stay spaces reserved for travellers who are passing through.

Children on the present unofficial lay-by site outside Adversale.

Politics

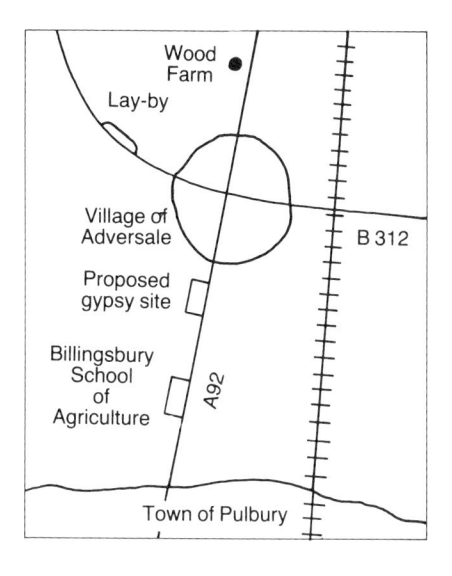

Background information

The 1968 Caravan Sites Act requires councils to provide official sites for travellers. One reason why the Act was passed was because gypsies were increasingly losing their traditional temporary sites on grass verges and common land. Another reason was that gypsies were switching to making a living from scrap metal work and many people wanted to put an end to scrap-littered roadside gypsy camps.

Councils providing official sites were given 'control powers' to remove all remaining gypsies on any unauthorised sites from the locality. By 1977 there were 109 permanent and 33 temporary official sites with 2,254 pitches. In 1980 central government provided £2.6 million to councils for 260 new pitches and in 1982 a further £3.8 million was committed for a further 380 new pitches.

(adapted from 'The Traveller-Gypsies' by Judith Okely, Cambridge University Press, 1983)

Those attending the Emergency Meeting of Adversale Parish Council

1 Mrs Palethorpe
(Proprietor of the Adversale Hotel) She is starting the AAGAG (Adversale Action Group Against Gypsies).

2 Mr Witty
(Owns new luxury home) He fears that the gypsy site will adversely affect the sale of houses in the village.

3 The Rev. Max Pointon
He believes it is his Christian duty to support the site but would rather not have it near his village.

4 Mrs Franklin
(Publican and chair of the Parish Council) She has welcomed travellers to her pub as customers and thinks the village should be positive, friendly and welcoming about the site.

5 Mr Burnikell
(Publican and ex-wrestler) He runs Adversale's other pub. He fears that gypsies could cause trouble and ruin his trade.

6 Chris Alexander
(Teacher and Parish Councillor) He teaches the Lee children who have been living on the lay-by site and attending Pulbury School for several years. He sees their need for a proper site with electricity and individual, fully-plumbed amenity blocks for each pitch.

7 John Davies
(Eccentric artist) He has come to the meeting because he enjoys a good argument. Could be convinced by a good cause.

8 Mr Whysall
(Antiques Dealer and Parish Councillor) He thinks the site would ruin the village.

9 Dr Marion Hunter
(Director of Billingsbury School of Agriculture) She has studied the plans for the site and noted that it will be surrounded by a 2-metre-high earth mound topped with closely planted conifers.

10 George Parperis
(Owns local building firm) He hopes he may get the contract for the construction of the site.

11 Davina Powell
(County Councillor) She owns considerable property in Pulbury and sees the isolated country site as the best solution to an awkward problem.

12 Jim Wright
(Farms at Wood Farm) He's fed up with travellers' caravans parked alongside his land.

13 Danny Lee
(Lays asphalt drives) He lives on lay-by site and wants his family to benefit from the new site's facilities. He may move on when his children have finished school.

14 Joan Radford
(Owns petrol station on A92) She has allowed Mr Lee to fill his old milk churn with water at her garage regularly.

This meeting is attended by other local residents, including the village police-woman.

D Discussion

Adopt one each of the above roles and then hold the Emergency Parish Council Meeting. Participants must put forward views which fit their roles as described above.

(This simulation exercise is adapted from *South Street Hostel Storm* and *Greenwood Gypsy Site*, both published by Community Service Volunteers, 237 Pentonville Road, London N1 9NJ. CSV produce a range of educational materials which are highly relevant to GCSE Sociology.)

The 1987 General Election

Source A: The Election result

	Percentage share of the vote	MPs elected
Conservative	42.2	375
Labour	30.8	229
Liberal/SDP	22.6	22
Welsh/Scots Nationalists	1.7	6
Northern Ireland Parties	2.2	17

Source B: Two advertisements from the campaign

IF THE TORIES HAD A SOUL, THEY'D SELL IT.

THE COUNTRY'S CRYING OUT FOR CHANGE. VOTE LABOUR.

LABOUR'S POLICY ON ARMS.

CONSERVATIVE
THE NEXT MOVE FORWARD

Source C: Private prosperity – the key to the Conservative victory

The dominant issues in the minds of the electors, according to surveys, before the 1987 election were the following: unemployment, the national health service, education, defence and pensions. On each of these issues, apart from defence, Labour's policies had more support than those of the Conservative party. Why then did the Conservatives win the election? The answer is that when replying to survey questions on the important issues respondents think of public problems; when voting they think of family fortunes. 'Prosperity' is not an issue or a problem, but a blessing. By a decisive 55 per cent to 27 per cent majority the public regarded the Conservatives as more likely to increase prosperity than the Labour party. Here, quite simply, lies the key to the Conservative victory.

Source D: The parties' shares of the vote among different groups of manual workers (percentages)

	Conservative	Labour	Liberal/SDP
The new working class			
Lives in South	46	28	26
Owner occupiers	44	32	24
Not union members	40	38	22
Works in private sector	38	39	23
The old working class			
Lives in North	29	57	15
Council tenants	25	57	18
Union members	30	48	22
Works in public sector	32	49	19

Source E: The gloomy picture for Labour – a regional class party

The Labour party has come to represent a declining segment of the working class – the traditional working class of the council estates, the public sector, industrial Scotland and the North, and the old industrial unions. Labour failed to attract the well-off and expanding working class of the new estates and the new service economy of the South. Labour was a party neither of one class nor of one nation. It has become a regional class party.

A survey of the 1987 election reinforces each of these conclusions. Labour remains the largest party among manual workers (42 per cent), but a minority party only 6 per cent ahead of the Conservatives. The political gulf between the traditional and the new working class remains. The Conservatives have majority support among manual workers in the South, owner-occupiers and among non-unionists. And the Conservatives are only 1 per cent behind Labour among manual workers who are employed in the private sector. Labour retains massive leads among the working class of Scotland and the North, among council tenants, trade unionists and among workers in the public sector.

In one important sense the picture is even gloomier for Labour now than at the 1983 election. Government policies are producing a steady expansion of the new working class and a reduction of the old. Council house sales, privatisation, the decline of manufacturing industry (on which the old unions are based) and the steady population drift to the South are continuing to expand the new working class and to reduce the old traditional working class.

(Sources A, C, D and E are adapted from 'Why Mrs Thatcher was returned with a landslide' by I. Crewe in *Social Studies Review*, September 1987)

Data-response questions

1 Using Source A:
   (a) What percentage of the vote did the Conservatives gain in 1987?
   (b) How many of the 650 seats in the House of Commons did the Conservatives capture?
2 What messages are put across by the two advertisements in Source B?
3 From Source C, which survey finding suggests 'the key to the Conservative victory'?
4 Using Source D:
   (a) What are the characteristics of the 'new' and of the 'old working class'?
   (b) What share of the working-class owner-occupiers' vote did the Conservatives gain?
5 According to Source E, why is the future gloomy for the Labour party?
6 Outline two social influences on voting behaviour not mentioned in the Sources.

Discussion

'It is a bad thing that performance by party leaders on television has become crucial to the outcome of British elections.'

Research suggestion

Hypothesis: Voters' concern with their own standard of living affects which party they vote for more than any other consideration.
Method: Give questionnaires to a cross-section of voters.

12 Deviance and crime

Deviance

Source **A**

THE Sun

Wednesday, November 4, 1987   20p   TODAY'S BINGO NUMBERS: PAGE 22

THE CONVICT

And they've even spelled poor Lester's name wrong

LESTER PIGGOTT poses in his usual poker-faced manner for photos ... but this time the snaps are for cameras in prison.

And Lester, the biggest star in British racing, even suffers the indignity of having his name spelt **WRONGLY**.

The man who took these jail mugshots of the crooked jockey—52 tomorrow—forgot to add the final "t" to the name known to millions.

The sporting legend, in striped prison shirt, clutched a black board with his jail number L15963 chalked across it.

He posed full-face and then sideways on for a profile shot.

Piggott is in "soft" Highpoint Prison in Suffolk.

COSY

He will serve his three-year sentence for a £3.1million tax fraud in the jail, just ten miles from his stables in Newmarket.

Lester the Lag has already been given a cosy cell and the cushiest jail job—distributing clothes and food.

Now he is looking forward to a birthday visit from his wife Susan, 48, and daughters Maureen and Tracy.

But prison chiefs have ruled out a special treat for their most famous prisoner—by ruling that the family **CANNOT** share a steak meal.

Portrait of a star in disgrace ... Lester Piggott's jail mugshot—with name spelled wrong.

Famous profile ... lag Lester

(from the *Sun*, 4 November 1987)

Deviance and crime

Source B

THE Sun
Thursday, November 12, 1987 — 20p — TODAY'S TV IS ON PAGE 14

PULPIT POOFS CAN STAY

Runcie... slammed prejudice

Church votes not to kick them out

THE Church of England voted NOT to ban gay priests yesterday ... despite hearing a shock indictment of perverts in the pulpit.

Church leaders snubbed a call by campaigning vicar Tony Higton to oust homosexuals, an estimated one in three of all clergymen.

Instead they voted by a massive 388 to 19 for a watered-down motion to condemn gay sex acts—but treat sinful clergy with "compassion".

The General Synod, the Church's ruling body, also issued a limp plea for gays to repent.

By JOHN KAY

CRUEL

It was backed by Archbishop of Canterbury, Robert Runcie, who said sex outside marriage was a sin, but homosexuality was "more difficult".

He insisted that to be gay by nature was still to be a full human being.

But the Rev Higton put before the Synod an amazing catalogue of outrageous behaviour by church gays in support of his case. He told of:

● The deranged priest who beat up a man trying to protect an unwilling victim of his gay lust.

● The Anglican theology college whose students were banned by another college because of their "rampant" homosexual practices.

● The child-molesting school rector who pinned up "explicit" gay propaganda in his church hall. After a conviction for child abuse he was appointed to another parish.

● The priest convicted of an act of gross indecency in a public toilet who was allowed to stay on—and then repeated the offence.

● The London meeting of Anglican gay priests where hard core male porn was for sale at a bookstall.

"The eyes of the world are on us," the Rev Higton claimed.

And if the church could not agree to ban gays when AIDS was sweeping the earth—"then God help us all."

To boos and hisses from the public in Westminster's Church House, Mr Higton slammed the promiscuity of gays.

But the Essex vicar denied he was leading a "witch-hunt".

The Rev Malcolm Johnson, of St Botolph's in the City of London, claimed gay relationships were part of the "splendid variety of God's creation".

He said he had recently buried a homosexual who had been faithful to his lover for 27 years.

"I thank God that such relationships are becoming more common."

The Rev Higton's supporters were heckled by a picket of gays and lesbians—led by failed Labour Parliamentary candidate Peter Tatchell.

Mr Tatchell stormed: "They are preaching a gospel of bigotry and intolerance. It gives succour and comfort to queerbashers everywhere."

Leading anti-child abuse campaigner Diana Core accused the Synod of "fudging the issue".

She said: "More and more vicars are molesting children sent to them in trust by their parents."

"The time has come for the Church to act."

(from the *Sun*, 12 November 1987)

Q Data-response questions

1 Using Source A:
  (a) What crime was Lester Piggott imprisoned for?
  (b) What attitude to Lester Piggott is expressed by the *Sun*'s article?
2 Give examples of acts which are
  (a) legal but socially deviant,
  (b) illegal but not deviant,
  (c) both deviant and illegal.
3 Using Source B:
  (a) What was the outcome of the debate of the Church of England's ruling body on the topic of gay clergy?
  (b) Make a list of all the words used that show the *Sun*'s prejudice against homosexuals.
4 What is the usefulness of this sort of source material to sociologists?

D Discussion

1 Is tax fraud a deviant as well as an illegal act?
2 'Imprisonment is an unsuitable punishment for the type of offence committed by Lester Piggott.'
3 'Drinking and driving, although illegal, is not considered by the majority of people to be a deviant or a truly criminal act.'

R Research suggestion

Hypothesis: The majority of Christians would be in favour of preventing practising homosexuals from becoming clergymen.
Method: Give a questionnaire to a sample of Christians.

Deviance and crime

Juvenile delinquency

Source A

THE recklessness of youth ravages our society. Thieving and crimes of violence against innocent citizens are such an everyday affair that they sometimes pass unnoticed ... except by their victims.
Tonight we focus on two cases where the lives of decent, ordinary people have been changed forever.
On the criminal calendar, the seriousness of each offence does not rate particularly high. But either of these crimes could happen in your street tonight. Your son or daughter simply couldn't do such things. Could they?
Bob Westerdale and Robert Taylor report.

CRIPPLED pensioner George Kelk hobbled home after being mugged by two young hooligans and burst into tears.

He cried from the shock of having his crutches kicked away from him in the very schoolyard in which he used to play happily as a child.

He cried too out of the sheer frustration of being a shadow of the man who years ago would have "belted the living daylights" out of his attackers.

For 40 years, in both steel and coal industries, he was a strong as an ox.

Now aged 77, George is riddled with arthritis, blind in one eye and short of breath through repeated, chronic bouts of bronchitis.

The great-grandfather has never felt the need to venture out of his native Yorkshire. He was born, brought up and worked in an area of Tinsley, Sheffield covering just a few miles.

It horrifies him how the neighbourhood has changed — and blames it mainly on the lack of discipline from parents.

Belted him

"We used to pull the piano out of the house and play it with the other kids in the street. Now they just run wild round here. What happened to me isn't all that unusual. But in my day it was unheard of.

"I was one of seven children. My mother used to wear a leather belt with a brass buckle and she would thrash us with it if we did anything wrong.

"I remember when our Bill pinched some taters from a shop and mum belted him all the way up Fitzmaurice Road until he showed her the shop and took them back.

"You'd never see that here now."

George's views were reinforced in a painful and degrading way. A few months ago he was walking from the Friendship pub to his tiny council home in Greenland Way when two yobs leaped on him.

"I can't see very well, but I think they must have been hidden anyway. They sent my sticks flying and held me on the floor. My knee hurt like hell as they pressed me down.

"They went through all my pockets taking £200. I always carried my savings around with me in case I came across a bargain.

George Kelk — muggers' victim who cried from shock when he got home

Muggers kicked away my crutches

"The buggers kicked away my crutches and even pinched my bus pass and club book. They ran off and I had a real job to get up. I rummaged around on my back-side until I found my sticks and managed to get home."

The after-effects were profound on George, both financially and mentally. He says he is often frightened in his own home and won't go out after dark.

"I always stop to look behind me whenever I'm outside. I don't like being near cheeky young kids in shops or at the pub. It worries me."

George insists the blame for juvenile delinquency lies in the lack of discipline in home and school, together with a shift in emphasis in policing.

"They are not brought up to respect the place they live in or their elders. At school we used to be in fear of doing anything wrong because we would get a good crack from the teacher's cane.

"I remember my wrist swelled up like a balloon when I was caned, but I didn't get in trouble again.

"Coppers regularly used to give us a hefty clip round the ear if we were being a nuisance, but they say they aren't allowed to do that now."

George recalls that work was normally available for young men in the thriving steel city in his day and feels some sympathy for those who cannot now find employment.

"They have too much time on their hands and turn to trouble. That doesn't explain why they are as wicked as they are though.

"I feel very bitter against the kids that robbed me. The police never found them. It scares me to think that I could so easily get mugged again. Next time I might not get away so lightly . . ."

(from the *Star*, a South Yorkshire newspaper, 9 December 1987)

Source B

Life on junk

THE NEW HEROIN USERS
Geoffrey Pearson
Blackwell £6.95 paperback/£17.50 hardback

GERRY STIMSON

It is still hard to comprehend the major disaster that has occurred. Unemployment, poor housing, the dismal lack of prospects for many young people are bad enough. The further legacy of these grim years is that heroin use has become a normal feature of our cities.

This is not to say that everyone uses it or that its use is condoned. But whereas a few years ago heroin was mainly confined to London's West End, and mostly used by the more eccentric, bohemian and transient, it is now something that most young people will come across. Heroin has become part of a way of life to the poor urban young in run-down industrial towns.

The "new" heroin users interviewed by Pearson and his colleagues in northern industrial cities were ordinary young people. They lived at home or in the neighbourhoods in which they grew up. Most were out of work. They had conventional values. Heroin was cheap entertainment. Wendy and Wayne from south Yorkshire explained that "a fiver [of heroin] gets three of us wiped out, donnit . . . against probably a tenner to go out supping." They were more likely to "chase the dragon" rather than inject it. This change marks a break with the earlier junkie subculture in which injecting was an important symbolic initiation—and deterrent.

This is not to argue that unemployment and deprivation cause addiction; but the conditions of many of our cities provide the right opportunities for heroin use to flourish. Many years ago, William Burroughs said that "junk wins by default." As Pearson puts it, heroin's advance is not like some cavalry charge but more like the slow trudge of a foot army. It slips in insidiously when there is a lack of other opportunities for people. It "creeps into their lives by stealth, slowly and imperceptibly."

No one forces anyone to use heroin. Pearson tries finally to demolish the myth of the "evil pusher at the school gates." The sad thing is that the first time someone is offered heroin it will be by a friend, a brother or a sister, always "by someone well known, liked and even loved." And no one sets out to be an addict. For Jack, aged 22, from Merseyside, "It was weird. I always said, everyone says like, I won't get hooked on it, and you never think you will." You slip through the "grey area" of casual use into habitual use.

The new heroin users are not lazy. Indeed, addiction gives a sense of purpose and an activity. Many years ago American research on street drug use showed that most heroin addicts have a hectic time "taking care of business." It is like that for today's addicts. Being "high" is only part of the day's work. There is the constant activity of raising money by theft or prostitution or by selling one's (or the family's) possessions. Next comes buying drugs, and then using them. After that the whole round starts again.

In this way heroin provides an alternative to work. Pearson argues that using heroin now provides the structures, routines, identity and self-esteem, friendships and social involvements once provided by work.

This makes it hard to stay off heroin. There is the problem of filling the place of heroin and providing a meaningful way of passing the time. Then, it is hard to escape temptation when it is as easy to buy heroin as it is to buy a packet of cigarettes. Wealth can provide the resources to move away from the area. This option isn't open to most of these young people. They have to learn to live without heroin in a neighbourhood where friends will still be using it.

The disaster that has overtaken us is that heroin is now entrenched in many parts of our cities. The problem with heroin, Pearson argues, is how to provide the possibility for people to "lead meaningful and rewarding lives and fashion effective identities in these run-down working class neighbourhoods."

(from *New Society*, 31 July 1987)

Data-response questions

1 Using Source A:
  (a) What particularly upset George Kelk about the attack he suffered?
  (b) Who does George blame for juvenile delinquency?
  (c) What long-term effects did the attack have on George?
2 Using Source B:
  (a) Who introduces most young addicts to heroin?
  (b) What are the characteristics of 'the New Heroin Users'?
  (c) How does heroin provide a meaningful alternative to work?
3 How do the sources differ as pieces of evidence?
4 What are the problems of using official figures on juvenile delinquency?

Discussion

Out of the 1,000 juvenile offenders who appeared before Sheffield's Juvenile Court in 1987, forty-two went into detention centres or youth custody. Why do many magistrates only give custodial sentences as a last resort?

Research suggestion

Hypothesis: The lives of old people are seriously affected by the fear of crime.
Method: Interview some old people.

The process of policing

Source A: Domestic violence and crime shrinkage

In 1984 and 1985 researchers examined the response of the Metropolitan Police in Hounslow and Holloway to 773 domestic incidents. 87 per cent were disputes between boyfriend and girlfriend, cohabitants or husband and wife. 2 per cent of cases resulted in men being charged and over 80 per cent of the cases of domestic violence were 'no-crimed'.

No-criming

This occurs when the police initially compile a crime report but then decide to drop the matter without pressing charges. This makes a nonsense of the accurate recording of criminal offences because no record of the offence is included in criminal statistics.

Why does no-criming occur?

Out of the 773 domestic disputes mentioned above, 61 assaults on wives were filed in crime reports. But 48 of these were dropped (no-crimed), 39 because the victim was unwilling to give evidence against the assailant.

The researchers found that the police avoid pressing charges in the following ways:

– they advised private prosecutions or civil remedies, even in cases of serious assault;
– they decided against arresting the man;
– they decided against charging the man for some time to allow a 'cooling-off period'.

From the point of view of the police it may be a waste of time to proceed if they expect the woman to withdraw her allegation.

From the woman's point of view, police inaction may leave her open to further violence. The deterrent effect of the law is lost if the police deliberately avoid immediate firm action such as arresting and/or charging the assailant. The woman also loses the protection of bail conditions – for example, an assailant may be released on condition that he does not visit the woman before the case comes to court.

(adapted from 'Police Response to Domestic Violence' by the Police Monitoring and Research Group of the London Strategic Policy Unit, 1986)

WIFE CAN'T LET BARLOW OFF FOR THUMPING HER

Tough-guy star must go to court, say cops

By NEIL SYSON

THE WIFE of tough-guy actor Stratford Johns has tried to drop an assault charge against her 18-stone husband—but police are insisting the case goes to court.

Johns, who played TV cop Charlie Barlow, is accused of causing actual bodily harm to his actress wife Nanette during a row at their home.

He allegedly hit Nanette, 52, who suffered minor cuts and bruises. She dialled 999 and 62-year-old Johns—former star of Z Cars and Softly, Softly—was arrested at his home in Wimbledon, South West London.

But Nanette said yesterday she telephoned Wimbledon police and they "agreed" to forget the matter. "It was a storm in a teacup," she said. "I have dropped the charge and Stratford will not be in court."

Her husband said: "It was just a row between a married couple, a typical theatrical row."

Evidence

But a Scotland Yard spokesman said: "In an incident like this, the aggrieved party has no power to drop the charge.

"Mr Johns will appear in court on July 12."

A legal expert said: "The police might decide to offer no evidence and the court would probably decide not to proceed with the case, particularly if Mrs Johns does not want to offer any evidence."

After being charged, Johns took his wife to a fancy dress party in London to celebrate the opening of Ken Russell's film Salome's Last Dance. Johns is playing evil King Herod.

The couple's 33-year marriage has been a turbulent one. In 1983, they got back together after a seven-year split.

(from the *Sun*, 30 June 1988)

Source B: Out on the beat

One evening D. J. Smith (the researcher) accompanied a group of uniformed officers carrying out a road block by a notorious council estate known to the police as 'the ratfarm'.

The local 'yobs' who were drinking in a pub opposite noticed what was going on and came out with their beer mugs to jeer at the police. The group of police officers included the home beat officer for the area, who felt a special responsibility, and who was losing face by being jeered at by his own 'yobs', on his own patch, in front of a whole party of other officers.

He and a fellow officer went off towards the pub, saying that they were going to 'sort out the yobs'. They would do this by 'winding up a yob' so that he would hit one of the officers and could then be arrested. But at this moment the Inspector who was organising the road blocks arrived in a car and got out. The 'yobs' in front of the pub jeered again, 'It's raining, you're going to get wet!', this time at the Inspector. He replied, 'So are you getting wet, but I'm getting paid for it', turned on his heel and walked away. When the home beat officer and his friend were about to reach the pub, the Inspector stopped them by giving them another task to perform.

The Inspector told D. J. Smith afterwards that if neither of them had been there these two PCs would have started a fight in order to be able to make arrests. The other officers who saw what happened said the same.

(adapted from *Police and People in London* by D. J. Smith and J. Gray, Gower, 1985)

Source C: Government blind eye to businessmen's crime wave?

A new report from the Low Pay Unit accuses the Government of 'turning a blind eye to what amounts to a crime wave of illegal underpayment'. The victims of this crime wave are many of the 2.25 million of the lowest-paid workers whose minimum pay levels are legally laid down by Wages Councils.

The report notes that the number of Wages Councils inspectors has been cut by more than half since the Conservatives came to power in 1979, while the number of social security fraud inspectors has risen dramatically.

While 31,524 workplaces were checked last year, the decline in the number of Wages Councils inspectors meant that fewer than 19,000 were visited. 4,443 employers were found to be illegally paying below the fixed minimum wage levels and employees were owed more than £1.2 million because of these underpayments.

Only nine prosecutions were brought against the 4,443 cases of illegal underpayment.

(adapted from the *Guardian*, 4 July 1988)

Data-response questions

1. Using Source A:
   (a) What is meant by 'no-criming'?
   (b) What percentage of domestic assaults in Holloway and Hounslow were no-crimed between 1984 and 1985?
   (c) Explain why no-criming of domestic assaults occurs.
2. Using Source B:
   (a) Why did the two officers set off to 'sort out the yobs'?
   (b) What, according to the Inspector, would have occurred if he had not given the two officers another task to perform?
3. Using Source C:
   (a) What is the accusation made by the Low Pay Unit?
   (b) What is the basis of this accusation?
4. 'The police (and Wages Councils inspectors) can choose whether or not to "create" crime.' Explain this statement with reference to all of the sources.

Discussion

'When called to an incident of wife-battering, the best course of action for the police to take is to arrest the husband.'

Research suggestion

Hypothesis: A considerable amount of crime is never reported.
Method: Give a questionnaire to a sample with questions such as, 'Have you ever been the victim of a crime? If so, did you report it?'

13 Wealth and poverty

The rich and the poor

Source A

Daily Mail
THURSDAY, FEBRUARY 25, 1988   22p

More and more are the self-made rich

MILLIONAIRES GALORE

Who's who of the 200 richest people in Britain — See Centre Pages

By JUSTIN DAVENPORT

BRITAIN is bursting with millionaires, a survey has revealed.

There are at least 20,000, including seven billionaires and 18 families or individuals worth more than £250million each.

(from the *Daily Mail*, 25 February 1988)

Source B: One view of the rich

Is envy ceasing to be Britain's national vice? That may be the most important conclusion to be drawn from *Money Magazine's* report on the 200 super-rich. For the surprising thing about the report is not so much that Britain now has 20,000 millionaires, as the public's reaction to their existence. Twenty years ago there would have been screams of jealous rage and demands for government action to curb the tendency of the few to pile up money and to keep it. To-day, however, the reaction has been much more varied and interesting. The main response is curiosity. For the first time there seems to be evidence that the Thatcher Revolution is not just affecting the British economy but is going much deeper and altering our way of looking at things. For it is of the essence of Thatcherism that wealth-creation is not something to be ashamed of. It is something to be welcomed, admired – and imitated.

What is so striking about the *Money Magazine* list is that two-thirds of those on it are self-made millionaires. Most people now get to millionaire status by their own efforts and the percentage is increasing rapidly. And these new fortunes are not just being made in the city. The new super-rich include entertainers and writers, sportsmen and media people, as well as industrialists and financiers.

Does this mean that envy is now dead in Britain? Alas no – not quite. On the same day the *Money Magazine* list was published, there was the Bishop of Manchester, the Right Reverend Stanley Booth-Clibborn protesting against wealth in the House of Lords. While student nurses were on £5,000 a year, he said, million-pound salaries for company chairmen were 'obscene'. I find it hard to believe that the bishop has given much thought to the matter. The ability to pile up a lot of money through legitimate enterprise is a sign not of greed but of efficiency, from which we all benefit, including nurses.

Most of the entrepreneurs on the list have got there by producing first-rate products, which have improved the quality of our lives. Then too, the bishop would surely realise that people with huge incomes cannot spend them all on themselves.

There is a limit to what a man can eat, drink and wear. The days when the rich ran vast establishments are over. Not many people live in palaces nowadays. Oddly enough, among the few who do are bishops.

People with very large incomes have no choice but to invest a large part of them. From that the community as a whole benefits, for investment means creating jobs. And investment is likely to be made far more shrewdly by individuals than by the state. Then too, the rich patronise the arts – and here again, the individual is more discriminating than publicly funded bodies like the Arts Council, run by committees giving away other people's money. Finally, and most important of all, the rich have a pleasing habit of giving their money away. For instance, most of the best schools and colleges in Britain have been founded and endowed by the rich.

(adapted from '200 Reasons Why We Are All Richer' by Paul Johnson in the *Daily Mail*, 26 February 1988)

Wealth and poverty

Source C: The numbers of the poor are increasing

There has been a substantial increase in the number of people in Britain who are poor, close to poverty or hard-pressed. The proportion of the population with incomes up to 40 per cent above supplementary benefit level increased from 22 per cent to 31 per cent between 1979–1983. Certainly, unemployment has been a major force for inequality; unemployment is closely related to social class. 1.5 per cent of professionals were unemployed in spring 1985, as were 3.5 per cent of class 2. But the proportions were 12.7 per cent for the unskilled, 9.6 per cent for the partly skilled and 9.6 per cent for the skilled.

Since 1980 state benefits have been cut. Unemployment benefit, for example, was cut in 1980 by 5 per cent. Two years later the earnings related supplement was abolished and benefits were made liable to tax. As a consequence the number of unemployed forced to rely solely on supplementary benefit increased more than 2.5 times from 675,000 to 1,770,000 between 1980 and 1986. A costing carried out by the House of Commons library showed that cuts in the rates of benefits for the unemployed totalled over £11,000 million between 1979 and 1986. By 1986 the cuts were worth £2,800 million per year.

(adapted from 'The Widening Gap' by the Labour Research Department, 1987)

Data-response questions

1 What political message is expressed in Source A?
2 Using Source B:
  (a) What, according to the writer, is the essence of Thatcherism?
  (b) What evidence does the writer give for the claim that Thatcherism is affecting our way of looking at things?
  (c) Which of the writer's arguments in defence of the rich do you think is the strongest?
  (d) The writer suggests that the bishop's complaint against the rich arises out of envy. What other feelings might have caused his response?
3 Using Source C:
  (a) Why have the numbers of the poor increased?
  (b) What was the total amount of the cuts in unemployment benefit between 1979 and 1986?

Discussion

Which point of view would you defend, that of Paul Johnson or that of the bishop whom he criticises?

Research suggestion

Hypothesis: While most people desire to be rich they do not envy the well-off.
Method: Give a questionnaire to a representative sample of children and adults. The questionnaire should contain questions relating to both parts of the hypothesis, that is, the desire to be rich and envy of the rich.

Unemployment and poverty

Source A: Homeless young people in London

Night train: The young homeless who sleep at the railway depot consider themselves lucky.

EVERY NIGHT at about 11.30, a group of young tramps march to the end of platform one at London Victoria Station, check that no one is following, and head off down the tracks. Half a mile away is the British Rail South Eastern depot where unlocked commuter trains provide a home for the night.

The railway tramps have come up with the best answer available to them to the capital's homelessness crisis. Compared with the estimated 2,000 young people who sleep rough in London every night, they consider themselves lucky.

The seats make comfortable beds, a residual heat lingers in the carriages, and there are plush wash rooms in first class. The cleaners who wake them up every morning are friendly. The British Transport Police are not, but their visits are less frequent.

There is also a nice irony in their choice of accommodation. Several of them only began visiting the depot when contractors working for BR's Property Board cleared down-and-outs from Charing Cross arches, their traditional home for 40 years, to build a multi-million pound office development.

It would be too comforting to say that the young people at Victoria are happy. Their condition is wretched, but they have developed an optimistic resilience, a way of managing. They are an élite group among the homeless, contemptuous of elderly alcoholics, but old and streetwise enough to avoid the drugs and prostitution rackets which entrap many runaway teenagers.

To Shelia McKechnie, the director of Shelter, their hopes are familiar and depressing.

"There are at least 50,000 homeless young people staying in squats, empty warehouses and hostels in London and it's going to get a lot worse," she said. "The social security Bill will cut off benefit to under 18-year-olds who won't go on YTS schemes, the housing Bill will push rents through the roof and the poll tax will encourage parents to chuck out grown up children.

"But all the young homeless people I meet are optimistic. They think that one day they're going to be pop stars or win the pools or that some one will stop them in the street and give them the keys to a BMW. It's the optimism of youth. They change when they're 30."

(from the *Independent*, 29 February 1988)

Source B: The meaning of poverty

A couple aged thirty and twenty-eight, with two children aged six and four were living in a £32-per-week council flat in East London. Housing benefit given by the local authority covered the rent, and the family also got £55 per week supplementary benefit plus £14 child benefit for the two children. Their income of £69 per week was just above the scale rates of supplementary benefit (£47.85 for a couple plus £10.10 for each child under 11 years, adding to a total of £68.05). The mother estimated that the income needed by the family to avoid poverty was £160 per week and the father £170 per week. They had no other form of income or assets. They had very few consumer durables. They had no telephone, iron, freezer or carpet. There were nine durables which they considered necessary but which they said they could not afford. There were a further six items in a list of housing facilities which they considered necessary and which they also could not afford. There was little space indoors and nowhere outdoors where young children could play safely. Although there was a central heating system it was not used, and was not on when the interviewer called that winter. It was a substandard council flat, with damp, broken floorboards and bad decoration.

The mother said she was in poor health, was not eating enough, had too little money, not enough sleep, and was worried about the family's flat and surroundings and about the future. She had gone without meals in the last fortnight to meet the needs of her family. There were days when 'the money ran out. We only had bread and butter and a couple of tins of soup – all we could afford'. On several of the dietary indicators the family were deprived. 'We don't have the right diet. We have mucky, greasy stuff all the time. I would like us to have more fresh food, fruit and meat, but can't afford it.' The same point kept resurfacing. When asked to define poverty she said: 'Going without things. You can't feed or clothe your kids or take them out. Eating bad food because that is all you can afford.'

(adapted from *Poverty and Labour in London*)

Source C: Unemployment in London

In 1987 London's economy is in deeper crisis than it has been for a hundred years. With over 400,000 unemployed the city has the largest concentration of unemployment of any city of the industrial world. Between 1971 and 1981 it lost 36 per cent of the jobs in manufacturing and, by 1985, a total of nearly half a-million jobs.

On the basis of data made available by the Government for 1983, it can be estimated that there are at least 300,000 people in London living below the Government's 'poverty line' or supplementary benefit standard. Another 600,000 receive supplementary benefit and a further 900,000 have incomes on the margins (with incomes from 1 per cent to 39 per cent above that level). The total is 1.8 million. A disproportionate number of these are women: women who look after children or other dependents unpaid and receive insufficient income; lone women with children, whether or not in paid employment; elderly pensioners, especially women living alone; and women with low earnings in households where total income is low relative to the supplementary benefit rates.

There is considerable evidence to show that current rates of social security are inadequate, especially for families with children. Also, there is much evidence of declining standards of service for social security claimants. Not surprisingly, the rise in unemployment has put considerable strain on the staff of social security offices.

(adapted from *Poverty and Labour in London* by P. Townsend, with P. Corrigan and Ute Kowarzik, Low Pay Unit, 1987)

Data-response questions

1 Using Source A:
   (a) According to Sheila McKechnie, how many homeless young people are there in London?
   (b) Give as many reasons as you can to explain why there are so many homeless young people in London.
2 Using Source B:
   (a) What is the total income of the family referred to in this source?
   (b) How might living in such conditions affect the children's educational progress?
   (c) What weekly income do you think a family with two children needs to avoid living in poverty? Show how you arrived at your figure by allocating so much per week for food, clothes and so on.
3 What is the difference between relative and absolute poverty?
4 Using Source C:
   (a) Why has unemployment increased in London over recent years?
   (b) How many of London's population are estimated to be poor or very near poverty?
5 What is meant by the 'poverty trap'?

Discussion

1 'A healthy society is one in which people accept responsibility for themselves and stand on their own two feet, therefore we must not encourage dependence on the state by making social security payments too high.'
2 'If the Government is serious about reducing crime then it ought to do something towards reducing unemployment, poverty and homelessness.'

Research suggestion

Compare the ideas and policies of the Conservative Party on the welfare state with those of the Labour Party.

To do this you could write to the Conservative Party's central office and the Labour Party headquarters to obtain information. You could also interview an MP or official from each party.

Poverty and health

(Sources A, B, C and D are adapted from *The Health Divide: Inequalities in Health in the 1980s*, a review prepared for the Health Education Council by Margaret Whitehead, 1987)

Source A: Recent trends

In the decade from 1971 to 1981 there was a fall in death rates in Britain, but these improvements in health were not experienced equally across the population. Non-manual groups experienced a much greater decline in death rates than manual groups, thus the gap between the two groups widened. Furthermore, death rates among women from coronary heart disease and lung cancer actually rose in manual groups over the ten-year period, while showing a substantial decline for non-manual women. There was also a widening gap between manual and non-manual groups in their rates of chronic sickness from 1974 to 1984.

Source B: Healthy eating and income groups

Food consumption by income group, Great Britain, 1984 (oz./person/week)

Income group	White bread	Brown bread	Sugar	Total fats	Fresh fruit	Fresh vegetables	Potatoes
A (richest 10%)	12	8	8	9	25	31	33
B (next 40%)	18	6	9	9	19	24	37
C (next 40%)	23	6	11	10	16	25	42
D (bottom 10%)	26	5	11	10	13	21	48

Source C: Deprivation and health in London

The Low Pay Unit's 1986 report 'Poverty and the London Labour Market' analysed material from the 1981 census for 755 wards in London. These wards were ranked for deprivation according to four indicators:

1 % of unemployed;
2 % of households with overcrowding;
3 % of households lacking a car;
4 % of households *not* owner-occupied.

Death rates (from 1979 to 1982) in the most deprived wards were found to be nearly double those of the least deprived wards.

Source D: The effects of income on health

In a study of 1,000 low-income people in the North of England in 1984 a quarter of respondents said that they did not have a main meal every day.

A 1986 study by dietitians calculated that a 'healthy diet' could cost up to 35 per cent more than the typical diet of a low-income family. Studies examining how mothers cope with the stress of caring for the family on a low income have found:

- sweets tend to be used as a quick and easy way of keeping children quiet on shopping trips and other stressful occasions;
- breast-feeding may be abandoned to allow more time for other members of the family;
- babies' milk may be mixed with cereal to help cope with crying and sleep problems;
- mothers may smoke as a way of easing tension without leaving the room.

It is commonly found in such studies that food is treated as a flexible item in the household budget (unlike rent and rates) and when money is short, food spending tends to get cut back. Families who economise on fuel risk making their homes not only cold but also damp and prone to condensation.

A study of low-income families on a 'hard to let' or 'sink' council estate in Liverpool concluded that the unsatisfactory housing conditions were contributing to high rates of

- infectious diseases (partly due to unhygienic mobile food vans used because the estate had no shops);
- respiratory disease (aggravated by ducted warm air heating and the practice of drying clothes indoors because of inadequate facilities);
- depression and mental illness.

Wealth and poverty

Source E

Meals for eight families living on supplementary benefit* in England and Scotland, 1980

	Adults' meals				Children's meals			
Family	Breakfast	Lunch	Tea	Supper	Breakfast	Lunch	Tea	Supper
1	nothing	toast, coffee	rice and fish	milk, biscuits	cereal, egg toast	School dinner sausage and beans	rice and fish	hot chocolate biscuits
2	nothing	fish and chips	nothing	nothing	cereal	pie and chips	nothing	bread and butter
3	tea	nothing	*Mother:* sandwich *Father:* sausage, egg and chips	*Father:* boiled egg and tea	toast and tea	School dinner soup and yogurt	sausage, egg and chips	toast and tea
4	drink	soup	drink	drink	cereal, toast	fish fingers and potatoes	soup	beans on toast
5	nothing	nothing	nothing	egg salad	cereal	School dinner	nothing	egg salad
6	coffee	nothing	spaghetti	tea	cereal	School dinner	spaghetti	tea and sandwich
7	nothing	egg and toast	nothing	nothing	cereal	beans on toast	sausage and chips	nothing
8	tea and toast	tea and biscuit	tea and toast	nothing	cereal	School dinner	fish fingers, sausage and beans	orange juice

* Now called Income Support.   (from *The Health of Nations* by the Open University U205 Course Team, 1985)

Q Data-response questions

1. Using Source A:
   (a) For which categories did death rates rise in the 1970s?
   (b) In what way has the 'health divide' widened?
2. Using Source B:
   (a) Give some clear examples of differences in food consumption between income groups.
   (b) Try to explain why, on average, poor people consume more sugar than rich people.
3. Using Source C:
   (a) What is meant by the death rate?
   (b) This research correlated (connected) data concerning local mortality (death) rates with data from the census. How was the census data used?
4. From Source D, give examples to illustrate how the following have been shown to affect the health of people on low incomes:
   (a) housing conditions,
   (b) stress on parents,
   (c) the juggling act of keeping within a very limited budget.
5. What evidence is there in Source E that poor families try to make ends meet by cutting back on food?

D Discussion

There are two major explanations for class inequalities in health:
(i) the materialist/structuralist explanation emphasises income and conditions such as the work and home environments,
(ii) the cultural/behavioural explanation stresses voluntary differences in lifestyle, such as physical exercise during leisure time and the fact that, of men in 1984, 26 per cent in Class V were heavy drinkers compared to 8 per cent in Class I.

Is poor diet mainly due to cultural behaviour or material deprivation?

R Research suggestion

Hypothesis: Higher income groups (for example owner-occupiers rather than tenants) are more likely to eat brown and wholemeal bread than the white, sliced variety.

Method: Interview a cross-section of people about their choice of bread and their housing tenure.

14 Work and leisure

What is work and how is it changing?

Source A: The four main employment sectors

The diagram shows the relative importance of the four main sectors of the formal economy according to the proportions of the workforce which they employ. Many statisticians break the economy down into three sectors but this analysis adds a 'quaternary sector' to show the growing importance of information technologies and of service industries which are basically involved in processing data, such as insurance.

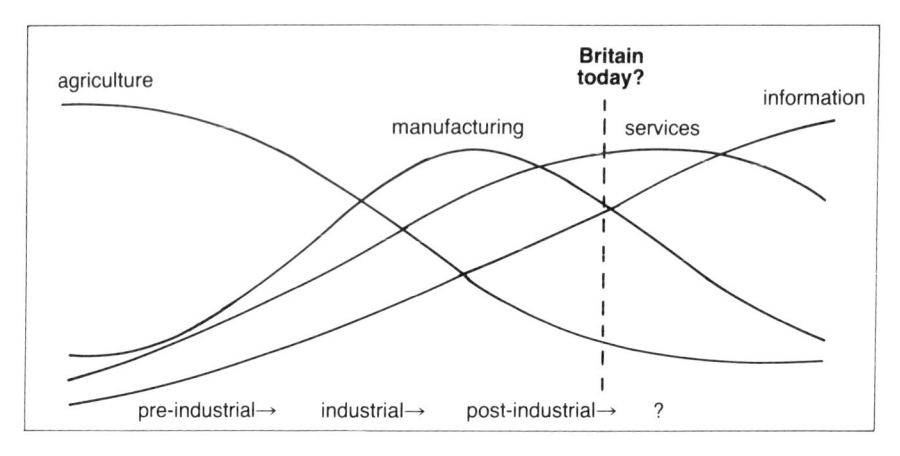

(from *Work in The Future: Alternatives to Unemployment* by John Osmond, Thorsons, 1986)

Source B: What is happening to work?

Though 76 per cent of those of working age are in the market for paid work, it may come as some surprise to learn that that amounts to only 35 per cent of the total UK population in full-time paid employment, with a further 8 per cent in part-time employment.

What are all the others doing with themselves? Women strongly claim that housework is indeed work, and children would be no less insistent that most schoolwork and homework are indeed work and not play. Further, those who are, as they say, gainfully employed hardly spend all their time in gainful employment.

In his book *Small Is Beautiful*, the late E. F. Schumacher calculated that, allowing for holidays, sickness or other absence, only about one-fifth of their total time is spent at the job. Much of what they do in their 'leisure' time – cooking, painting the house, looking after the children, travelling to and from work – is indistinguishable from what other people do for pay; it certainly seems odd to call it leisure just because the worker is doing it in his or her 'time off'.

The four economies
What distinguishes different kinds of work is not different kinds of *tasks* but the different kinds of relationships within which they are performed. Four may be distinguished:

1 The formal economy is the world of paid employment. Jobs are performed because someone is prepared to pay someone else to do them. The deal is: work in exchange for cash. Other motives, such as loyalty, self-fulfilment, service or doing someone a good turn, may abound, but the basic deal is the work/cash contract.

2 The household economy concerns work done within the home for fellow members of the household, usually spouses, children or parents. This work is done not for money but out of commitment to the other members or to the family unit as such. It may be hoped that adult beneficiaries of such labour will put in as much as they get, but there is no such expectation with children and sick, disabled and elderly adult beneficiaries.

3 The informal economy concerns unpaid work for non-family, non-household, people. Examples are: voluntary work, doing a favour for a mate, looking in on the old lady two doors down or cooking dinner for her, swopping garden produce with neighbours, standing in the local election and holding a dinner party.

Though some rough element of exchange may exist (as with hostesses who expect their guests to return the dinner invitation or with gardeners and their produce), the dominant relationships are those of friendship, neighbourliness, love, loyalty, generosity and pleasure in sharing; or perhaps of influence, status and power.

4 The black economy involves paid work that is not declared to the Inland Revenue (which collects income tax). The black economy proceeds according to rules that are a mixture of the formal and informal economies. Some payment for the job is involved, but this is usually way below the formal market rate not only because of the tax saved but also because the worker is often doing the job partly as a favour, to return a favour, or to lend a helping hand.

(adapted from *Hope On The Dole* by Tony Walters, SPCK, 1985)

Source C: Four aspects of economic restructuring

Jobs in Britain have recently been affected by major changes in the structure of the economy.

1 Sectoral shifts in employment

(a) The decline in manufacturing jobs From the mid-1960s to the mid-1980s manufacturing fell from over 33 per cent to around 25 per cent of all jobs. Between 1982 and 1986 manufacturing output rose but manufacturing jobs fell by a further 400,000: a situation of 'jobless growth'.

(b) The rise in service jobs By the mid-1980s the service sector accounted for nearly 66 per cent of employment. But while the growth in service sector employment to some extent compensates for the decline in jobs in manufacturing, the jobs created are often filled by women working part-time, rather than by the predominantly male labour force displaced by the shrinkage of manufacturing employment.

2 Locational shifts in employment

The West Midlands was a post-war boom area but it has seen rising unemployment in the 1980s. The result is that the prosperous South has shrunk as the depressed North has moved further South. But the North/South divide is misleading. There are pockets of prosperity in the North and there is high unemployment in inner-London. A general trend has been the 'decentralisation' of employment away from large urban centres.

3 Male and female employment

Between 1974 and 1984 the number of full-time male and female employees declined by around 10 per cent, while the number of women in part-time work increased by 22 per cent. Over the same period, part-time female employment fell in many areas of manufacturing (for example, down 54 per cent in textiles) but rose in some parts of the service sector (for example, 61 per cent in hotels and catering).

In *Divisions of Labour* (1984) R. E. Pahl has noted how the wives of men in work are around twice as likely to be in employment as the wives of the unemployed. This is largely because wives' earnings are offset against husbands' social security entitlements. Consequently a division is opening up between households with two (or more) wage-earners and those with none, who are consequently almost wholly dependent on state benefits.

4 The restructuring of labour markets and employment conditions

Many employers have 'slimmed down' their labour forces in the 1980s and have broken down established work practices and manning arrangements. Alongside this smaller, more flexible, permanent workforce there has been substantial growth in temporary work, subcontracting and short-term contracts.

(adapted from *Inside British Society* by G. A. Causer, Wheatsheaf, 1987)

Data-response questions

1 Using Source A, describe the trends in employment in each of the four sectors of the economy.
2 Using Source B:
   (a) What proportion of the total UK population is in full-time paid employment?
   (b) In which of the four economies do the following workers belong?
       (i) a burglar, (ii) a police constable, (iii) a Samaritan or WRVS lady, (iv) a middle-aged woman who looks after her elderly mother.
   (c) Which non-financial motives for working are likely in each of the four economies?
3 Using Source C:
   (a) How is it that manufacturing jobs have fallen while, at the same time, manufacturing output has risen?
   (b) Why is the idea of the North/South divide misleading?
   (c) Outline the 'division' to which Pahl has drawn attention.

Discussion

'Someone who is unable to find paid employment in the formal economy can easily find work to do in the non-formal economies.'

Research suggestion

Hypothesis: A larger minority of young workers would like to be self-employed (if given the right opportunities) than older workers.
Method: Interview samples of young and older workers about their attitudes to self-employment.

Occupations

Source **A**: A day in the life of a teacher (written by Julie King)

Julie King at work

'I am the Head of Biology and Head of Year in a multicultural, single sex, Girls' Comprehensive School in Birmingham. I enjoy my work because I am forever facing new challenges. It is demanding, stressful and at times hectic. I try to use my sense of humour to keep things in perspective. To describe a typical day is difficult, since no two days are the same. I will describe yesterday to give you an idea.

I arrive at school at 8.30 am – this gives me time to prepare things. I check I have ordered all the practical apparatus needed for the day and talk to the laboratory technician about any changes. I then have a coffee and a chat with colleagues in my department. We are disturbed by a knock on the door: a pupil wants to give me £25 in coins that she has raised during the 'red nosed conga' that I organised for Comic Relief Day. I thank her and lock the money in my filing cabinet. It's my year's assembly this morning so I dash upstairs to let the technician know where to put the TV and video.

We have a staff meeting for 10 minutes every morning. I announce that I have organised a group of girls to teach the staff some words and phrases in Punjabi. My assembly is about changes at puberty and adolescence. I show a part of a video and hold a discussion on this topic. This goes well and so I feel on a high as I rush up to my first lesson which is a fifth year practice assessment. These assessments are a bit of a nightmare as I have so many check points to observe in a double lesson.

Break is at 10.40 am – I get a message from the secretary saying that a social worker rang and could I telephone her as soon as possible. A girl in my year has been taken off the 'at risk' register for child abuse and I am being asked to monitor the situation carefully. I find the girl's form tutor to relay the message and we discuss the issue until the end of break.

11.00 am – another double lesson – fourth year biology – we are doing digestion. In groups of four the pupils are given large sheets of paper to use to draw the outline of the human body. They collect packs of life size organs of the digestive system to fit where they think they should go. I walk round and smile to myself at the misplaced organs.

12.05 to 12.10 we have a five minute break. I am looking forward to a cup of coffee when I am telephoned by the headteacher who asks me to report to the office as a parent I was expecting later has arrived early. This meeting is about a pupil who was suspended last week for fighting. We make it clear that the school does not tolerate violent behaviour and that if it happens again the girl will have to attend another school. We draw up a contract which is signed by the pupil, her mother and her social worker. I am pleased to have this pupil back because she is a bright and pleasant child despite having a temper which she finds difficult to control. After her mother and social worker have left we sit and talk. She says she is pleased to be back in school. I put her on a daily report.

1.20 – lunch time – I eat a meal quickly, chatting with colleagues and then attend a meeting with other Year Heads and the Deputy Head. We are discussing reports and profiles. At 2.20 the bell rings for afternoon school. I register a form for one of my tutors who has a theatre group in school. The last double lesson is with a fifth year B. Tec group. We are looking at the hazards of smoking.

We examine photographs of lungs with cancer in them and form discussion groups exploring the reasons why people smoke, etc.

3.35 pm – end of school. The re-admitted pupil brings her daily report for me to read and sign. She had excellent for every lesson and she looks pleased with herself. I have another meeting with my form tutors to plan our tutorial programme for the next few weeks and evaluate what we have done so far. Meeting finishes at 5.00 pm. I have a pile of books I must mark by tomorrow. I mark a few but I have to leave at 5.30 pm because the school is locked. I take the marking home with me.

At home I feel exhausted, drained and rather harassed at the thought of spending the evening marking, but this is balanced with feelings of job satisfaction – it's been a productive, lively day.'

Work and leisure

Source B: A day in the life of an assistant purser on Sealink British Ferries

THE P & O ferry dispute tomorrow enters its eleventh week. At issue is the company's demand for new working arrangements. JOHN POLLARD is an assistant purser on Sealink British Ferries, where similar shift schemes are already in operation. Here he describes a day in his working life.

FERRY CREWS PAY THE PRICE OF PRESSURE

by JOHN POLLARD

06.45 I join my vessel. During the initial crossing from Folkestone to Boulogne I and my colleagues grab a 15-minute break for breakfast.

10.30 We discharge at Boulogne and immediately embark passengers as soon as the ship is cleared of rubbish etc. This crossing is train-connected so we may expect anything from 100 to 800 foot-passengers. My colleague and I collect their tickets and issue them with the new boarding passes. At the other end of the vessel cars, coaches and freight are being loaded. We put our figures together to arrive at the total passenger figure. Forty-five minutes after arriving, we sail.

11.30 Paperwork, manifests, answering questions and giving information. By midday the second trip of the day is over. I take the 'papers' ashore and return to the ship ready to embark for the next sailing.

13.15 Another train. Repeat operation. We are late, due to large loads and extra traffic — in this case from the P & O dispute.

16.00 We have emptied the vessel of passengers. It is lunchtime. We have half an hour. We have been on duty since quarter to seven in the morning and apart from our breakfast we have had no more than the odd five-minute break for a coffee. We only have to cross the channel three more times! We are halfway there!

17.00 Our fourth trip. In normal circumstances on this trip we receive the English 'day-tripper', 97 per cent wonderful, 3 per cent ghastly. We can tolerate some noise and buffoonery, but abuse and aggressiveness after partaking of French wine get to us. The British can get extremely stupid (this is tolerable) and very nasty. One of my colleagues leapt into Boulogne Harbour to save a young man who was not only unable to swim but was drunk as well. No 'thank you' note later. He could have drowned while his party looked on laughing. Another colleague had a rather tender part of his anatomy squeezed and his ear cuffed because he wanted to see the gentleman's(?) ticket. *C'est la vie!*

19.00 We arrive back in Folkestone and another quick 'turn-round'. Mostly freight, but a couple of coaches and a few cars. We catch up with paperwork which has been neglected due to the pressure of business. Life becomes more staid and gentle, but there is still enough to keep us busy. We have been at our place of work now for 14 hours with no real break.

22.30 We depart for our home port where we can enjoy our six-hour rest.

01.00 By the time the ship is tied up we have worked for 18 hours. Most of us can go home to sleep in our own beds. Should the weather be bad, however, many of the crew have to remain on board, for which they receive £1 an hour. True, their services may not be required, but they are still on duty. Those crew members required for watch-keeping are paid extra since they are required to walk around the vessel at intervals and cannot sleep during this period for more than the odd hour.

06.45 Rejoin vessel. The officers perform this turn of duty one week on, one week off, except during the summer when it is two on, one off. The ratings do two on, one off all year round. We all have a 19-day summer annual leave period. We all work weekends and bank holidays and this year my crew will be working on Boxing Day. My salary, including all increments, amounts to approximately £13,000 per annum.

I don't criticise the company about all this — they've always been good employers to me. I'm just saying that these shifts take us to the limit of what's humanly possible.

(from the *Observer*, 17 April 1988)

Q Data-response questions

1 Using Source A:
 (a) Apart from the pupils she teaches in lesson times, list all the people with whom Julie King spent time during the typical working day which she describes.
 (b) What type of activities 'eat into' her time during breaks and before and after the lessons of the day?
 (c) What do you suppose are the main advantages and disadvantages of such a job?

2 Using Source B:
 (a) Describe the sorts of duties undertaken by an assistant purser on a cross-channel ferry.
 (b) How does the shift system operate for ratings (non-officers) on Sealink British Ferries?
 (c) How might the demands of such a shift system affect a worker's social life, family and health?

D Discussion

'Quite apart from financial considerations, our working lives inevitably influence, and quite often dominate, our non-working lives.'

R Research suggestion

Hypothesis: The unpaid job of being a housewife compares unfavourably with many occupations, in many ways.

Method: Ask several housewives and a number of people in paid work to keep an hour-by-hour record of a typical working day. Go through their record asking them what proportion of the working day was (a) monotonous and boring; (b) stressful – causing pressure; (c) free time for eating, drinking, relaxing or being sociable.

Working conditions, leisure and class

Source A: Inequality at work

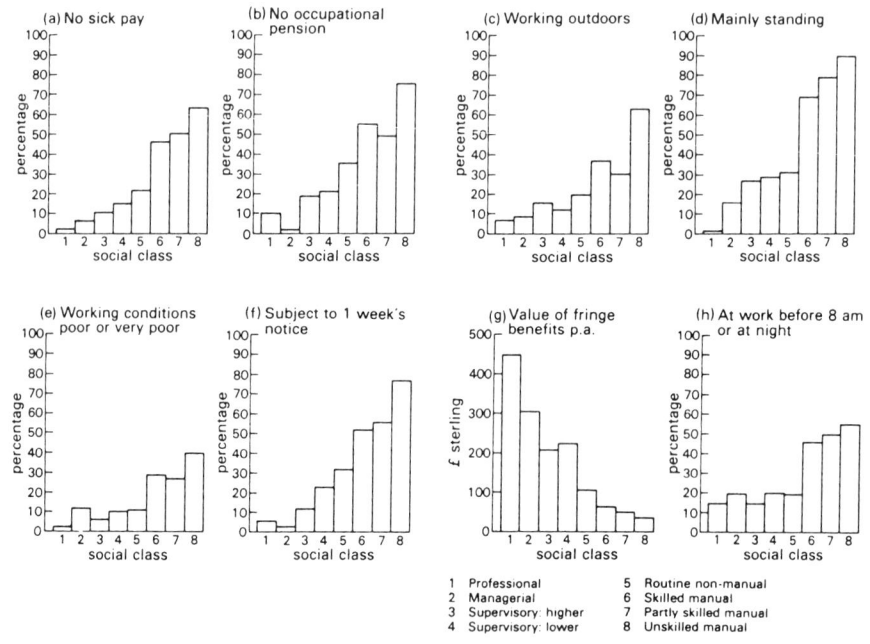

(a) No sick pay
(b) No occupational pension
(c) Working outdoors
(d) Mainly standing
(e) Working conditions poor or very poor
(f) Subject to 1 week's notice
(g) Value of fringe benefits p.a.
(h) At work before 8 am or at night

1 Professional
2 Managerial
3 Supervisory: higher
4 Supervisory: lower
5 Routine non-manual
6 Skilled manual
7 Partly skilled manual
8 Unskilled manual

(from *Poverty in the United Kingdom* by P. Townsend, Penguin Books, 1979)

Source B: Holidays of four or more nights away from home, by class[1]

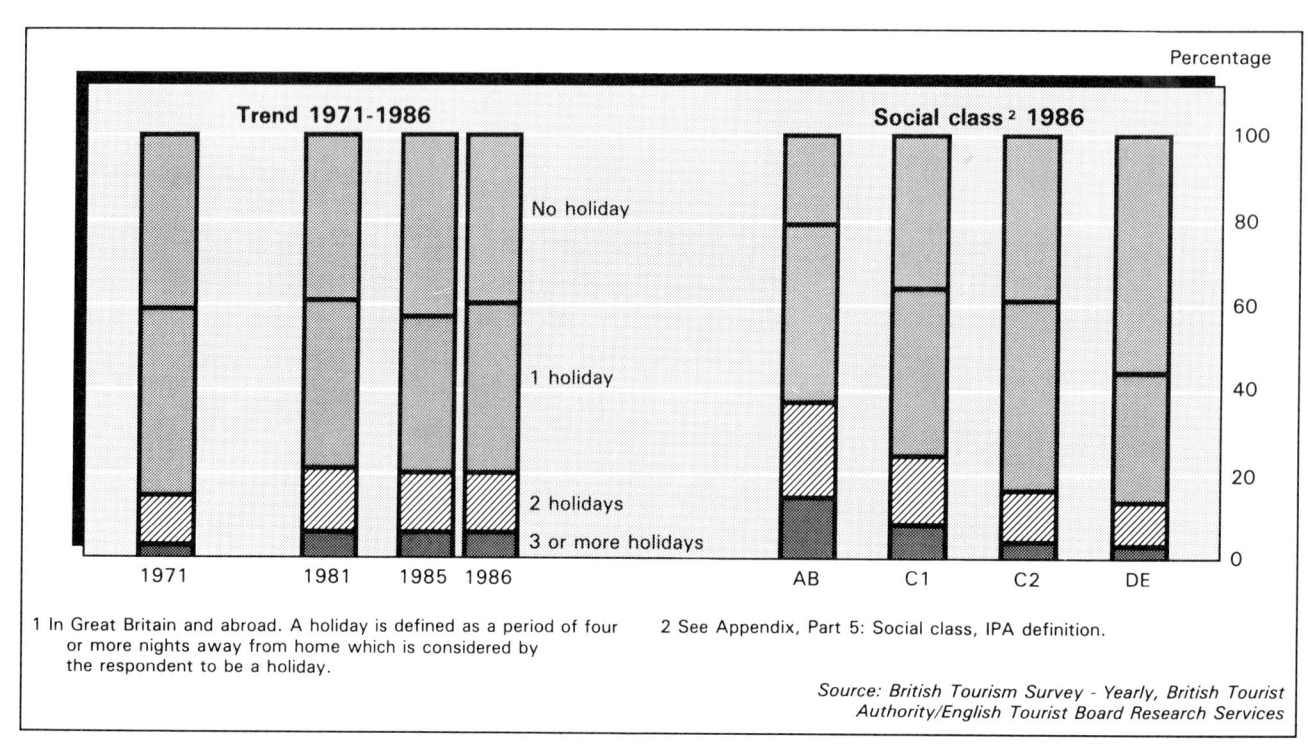

Trend 1971–1986 — 1971, 1981, 1985, 1986
Social class[2] 1986 — AB, C1, C2, DE

Categories: No holiday, 1 holiday, 2 holidays, 3 or more holidays

1 In Great Britain and abroad. A holiday is defined as a period of four or more nights away from home which is considered by the respondent to be a holiday.
2 See Appendix, Part 5: Social class, IPA definition.

Source: British Tourism Survey - Yearly, British Tourist Authority/English Tourist Board Research Services

(from *Social Trends*, 1988)

Source C: Television viewing, by class

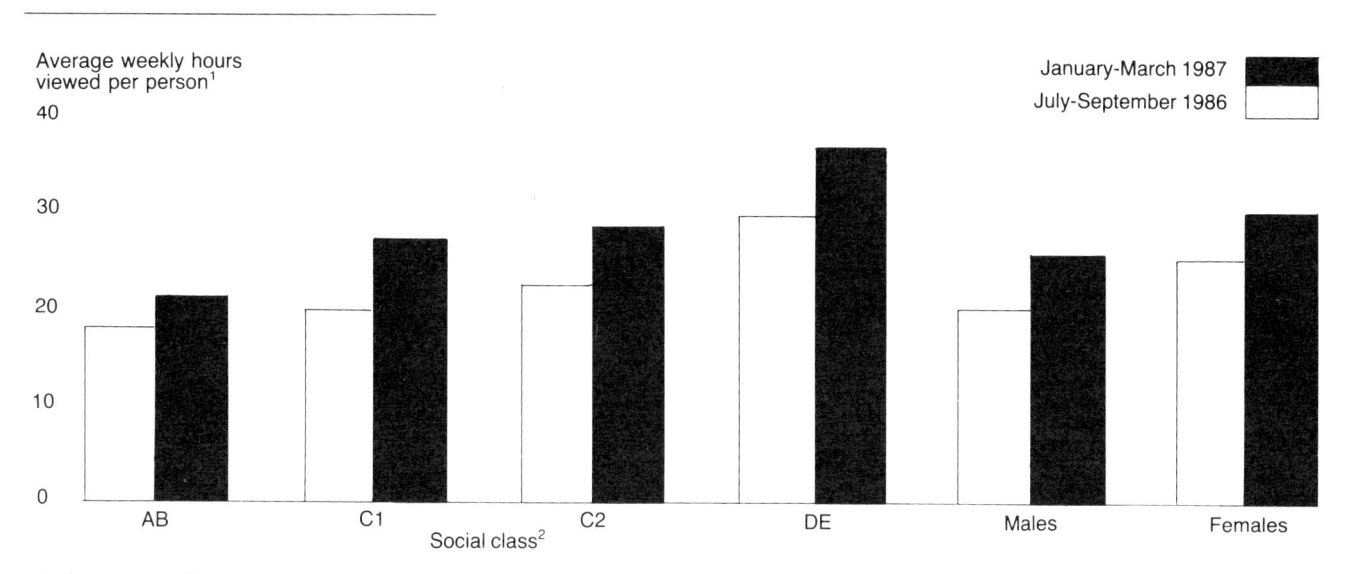

Average weekly hours viewed per person[1]

January-March 1987
July-September 1986

(Bar chart showing average weekly hours of television viewing by social class AB, C1, C2, DE, and by Males and Females)

Social class[2]

1 Persons aged 4 or over.
2 See Appendix, Part 5: Social class, IPA definition.

Source: Broadcasting Audience Research Board; Audits of Great Britain

(from *Social Trends*, 1988)

Social class: Institute of Practitioners in Advertising (IPA) definition

Social class categories are based on head of household's occupation as follows:

Class A	Higher managerial, administrative, or professional
Class B	Intermediate managerial, administrative, or professional
Class C1	Supervisory or clerical, and junior managerial, administrative, or professional
Class C2	Skilled manual workers
Class D	Semi and unskilled manual workers
Class E	State pensioners or widows (no other earners), casual or lowest grade workers, or long-term unemployed

Key for Sources B and C

Q Data-response questions

1 Using Source A:
   (a) What percentage of unskilled manual workers spend their time at work 'mainly standing'?
   (b) Which group gets the most fringe benefits?
   (c) What is meant by fringe benefits? Give two examples.
   (d) Which of the different conditions at work might affect (i) leisure and (ii) health. Explain your answer.
2 Using Source B, compare the percentages of classes AB and DE having no holidays away from home. Give figures.
3 What do Sources B and C tell us about the leisure patterns of different social classes?

D Discussion

What might be meant by 'working conditions poor or very poor'?

R Research suggestion

Hypothesis: The disadvantages of shift work outweigh the advantages.
Method: Interview a number of shift-workers.

The trade unions

Source A: Will occupational changes lead to a decline in union power?

[Many believe that the decline in manufacturing industries where unions are well organised and the rise in new service employment where they are poorly organised indicates that the power of unions will inevitably decline.] As the labour editor of *The Financial Times* rather crudely puts it: 'Britain's unions have failed to crack these new industries – failed to follow the work. Employment has shifted massively from manufacturing, hit hard by recession, to the private sector service industries . . . such as tourism, hotels and restaurants . . . The unions have not followed suit.'

John Edmonds [the General Secretary of the General, Municipal and Boilerworkers' Union] expresses essentially the same idea:

> 'We must accept that within the next decade the trade unions are not going to be in a position to force contract cleaners, for example, to pay reasonable pay and conditions through traditional trade union organisation. We are not going to have effective trade union organisation in every large hotel in the country . . . The whole private service area, particularly leisure, isn't well organised and is likely to remain significantly unorganised for all sorts of structural reasons . . . If you have an industry where the workforce is highly mobile, where they are not attached to any particular employer for any length of time, then the organisational difficulties are very substantial indeed. It is obviously more difficult to organise there than it is in a factory of 500 people who have relatively long service records.'

There are a number of obvious points that can be made about Edmonds' claims. Groups such as contract cleaners could often easily be organised if the unions in organised workplaces would black [refuse to deal with] non-union firms; they do not do so because people like Edmonds are too frightened to confront the Tory laws.

Over the years union activists have succeeded in organising industries such as the print [industry] where workplaces are, on average, much smaller than in the big hotels or the big chain stores. . . .

It is not true that all hotel, catering, distribution or 'leisure' employees are continually changing jobs; usually there are groups of permanent workers who can maintain continuing organisation, as is shown by the fact that there have been successful attempts at unionisation.

But there is a more central fallacy than any of these in Edmonds' approach: the fact that he concludes from the failure of the unions to build in such a growth area that therefore union strength is bound to decline generally. Union strength does not just depend on how many workers are organised, but on the ability to take economically effective action. And even if the hotel, catering, retail and leisure sectors remain weakly organised, other sectors do retain mass potential strength.

(from *The Changing Working Class* by A. Callinicos and C. Harman, Bookmarks, 1987)

Source B

'Death' of the unions

CURBS UNDER MAGGIE ARE WEAKENING THEIR GRIP

By PAUL EASTHAM

THE unions' grip on British industry has finally been broken after 150 years, a survey reveals.

Only 42 per cent of the workforce now choose to be in a union, it says.

A series of 'hammer blows' by the Tories under Mrs Thatcher cost them three million members and deprived them of influence in the corridors of power, according to the journal Personnel Management.

However, in another report, some of the country's industrial heads say curbs on unions have gone far enough, and they urge the Government not to 'go in for the kill' with ever tougher legislation.

They feel the movement, with certain reforms, could make a more positive contribution to the growth and prosperity of industry, says a report in Chief Executive magazine.

The Personnel Management report reveals that unions admitted in a secret paper to the TUC's current review body that although the booming economy is now increasing the number of people in work by 150,000 a year, union membership is falling by 250,000 a year.

Author Philip Bassett, says: 'Non-unionism is now dominant in Britain. Most employees are no longer union members.

'The hammer blows to the unions are deeply familiar; three million members lost, elbowed from the Whitehall corridors of power, shunted out of the highly-unionised manufacturing citadels of the North, Midlands and Scotland. Nothing much looks likely to change in the future either,' says Mr Bassett, labour editor of the Financial Times.

Booming

But more ominously for the unions is the fact they are losing the battle for members in the fastest growing firms such as high-tech, electronics, service companies and small businesses.

In Scotland 85 per cent of small businesses do not allow unions, and 51 per cent of the booming 'Silicon Glen' electronics plants are non union.

In Milton Keynes, Buckinghamshire, Britain's fastest growing city, 3,500 new jobs have been created in each of the past three years, but union chiefs admit non membership is 80 per cent.

Britain's biggest union the transport workers, admits membership losses in the key car, chemicals, construction and transport industries has been more than double the loss of jobs through unemployment in these sectors.

(from the *Daily Mail*, 29 February 1988)

Q Data-response questions

1 Using Source A:
   (a) Give two reasons put forward for the claim that union power will decline in the future.
   (b) Give two reasons put forward for the claim that it is not necessarily the case that union power will decline.
   (c) Which claim do you find the most convincing? Explain your answer fully.
2 What benefits do employees gain from belonging to a union?
3 Using Source B:
   (a) What is the level of union membership in growth areas such as Milton Keynes and 'Silicon Glen'?
   (b) What does the use of expressions such as 'weakening their grip' tell us about the bias of the source?
   (c) Is the headline justified by the evidence in the article?

D Discussion

'Unions need to change their image if they are to succeed in attracting new members from amongst young employees.'

R Research suggestion

Carry out research into the reasons why some employees belong to a union and why some do not. Questionnaires and in-depth interviews are the most suitable methods to use in this research.

Answers to the quiz about working women on p. 26	1 b	5 d	9 c	13 T
	2 d	6 T	10 d	14 c
	3 T	7 d,f,g,h	11 a	15 b
	4 d	8 T	12 T	

Answers to the youth cults 'matching-up' exercise on p. 30	1 F	5 G
	2 D	6 B
	3 H	7 A
	4 C	8 E

Acknowledgements

We are grateful to the following for permission to reproduce photographs and copyright material:

BBC Copyright ©, page 27; Camera Press, page 50 (Colin Davey); Conservative Party, page 90 *right;* Daily Express, page 80 *above;* Daily Mirror, page 80 *centre;* Sally & Richard Greenhill, pages 60, 61, 88; Labour Party, page 90 *left;* Mail Newspapers plc, pages 28 (photo: Solo Syndication), 32 *below,* 55 (photo: Solo Syndication); Maggie Murray/Format, page 40 (2); The Observer Ltd, page 87 (photo: John Reardon); Popperfoto, page 76 (2); Rex Features, page 70; The Shaftesbury Society, page 74 *left; Spare Rib,* July 1987, page 26 *above;* Times Newspapers Ltd, pages 52, 64.
Cover: (cartoon) from *New Society* 3.4.87.

Philip Allan Ltd for adapted extracts from article 'General Election 1987' by J. Benyon *Social Studies Review* Nov. 1987 & extracts from article 'Why Mrs Thatcher was returned with a Landslide' by Ivor Crewe *Social Studies Review* Vol. 3, No. 1 Sept. 1987; the Author, Simon Beavis for an adapted version of his article 'Government turns blind eye to businessmen's crime wave' *The Guardian* 4.7.88; Basil Blackwell for summarised & adapted extracts from *The Making of a Moonie* (1984) by E. Barker & *Real Wicked Guy* (1983) by R. Kerridge; Bookmarks for extracts from *The Changing Working Class* by Alex Callinicos & Chris Harman; Cambridge University Press for adapted extracts from *The Traveller-Gypsies* (1983) by J. Okely; the Author, John Cunningham for an adapted extract from his article on 'Professor Neville Butler's Survey . . .' *The Guardian* 29.12.87; English Centre for an adapted extract from *The English Curriculum: Gender* by Margaret Sandra; Gower Publishing Group for adapted extracts from *Green and Pleasant Land* by H. Newby & *Police and People in London* by D. J. Smith & J. Gray; International Thomson Publishing Services Ltd for an adapted extract from *Tales out of School* by R. White & D. Brockington; IPC Magazines Ltd for an adapted extract from article by A. Kelly *New Scientist* 20.5.82; Labour Research Department for adapted extracts from 'Healthy & Wealthy' p. 25 *Labour Research* Vol. 76, No. 1. & 'The Widening Gap' p. 110 *Labour Research Dept* 1987; Longman Group UK Ltd for an adapted extract from *An Economic & Social History of Britain 1760–1970* (1987) by T. Mays; Low Pay Unit for adapted extracts from *Poverty & Labour in London* (1987) by P. Townsend; National Council for One Parent Families for an adapted extract from *Illigitimate* edited by D. Derrick, © One Parent Families 1986; Newspaper Publishing Plc for article 'The myth exploded: schools really do matter' by Peter Wilby *The Independent* 24.3.88; The Observer Ltd for an extract from the article 'Two Nations Even at School' by Chris Curling *The Observer* 7.2.88; Simon & Schuster Ltd for adapted extracts by G. Allen, A. M. Rees, G. A. Causer from *Inside British Society* ed. G. A. Causer (Wheatsheaf 1987); The Society for Promoting Christian Knowledge for an adapted extract from *Hope on the Dole* by Tony Walter, © J. A. Walter 1985; Solo Syndication & Literary Agency for an adapted extract from article '200 reasons why we are all richer' by P. Johnson *Daily Mail* 26.2.88. © Mail Newspapers Plc; Novosti Press Agency/Soviet Weekly for adapted article by Tretyakov in *Soviet Weekly* 6.2.88; Statesman & Nation Pubg. Co Ltd for adapted extracts from articles by A. Mitchinson *New Society* 5.2.88, Janet Finch *New Society* 20.3.87, J. Burgoyne *New Society* 10.4.87, L. Morris *New Society* 3.4.87, C. Ward *New Society* 4.3.88, 'Society Today' insert pp ii–iii *New Society* 17.3.83, D. Hay *New Society* 17.4.87 & G. Heald *New Society* 17.3.83; The Spectator Ltd for extract from the article 'Sexist practices at the table' by Nigella Lawson *The Spectator* 14.11.87; Times Newspapers Ltd for an extract from an article by M. Whorle p. C9 *The Sunday Times* 31.1.87. © Times Newspapers Ltd 1987.

We have unfortunately been unable to trace the copyright holders of extracts from *The Subversive Family* by F. Mount, *Police Monitoring & Research Group Briefing Paper 1 & Policing London* and would appreciate any information that would enable us to do so.